Nostalgic Memor
of
KINGSTON UPON HULL

First published in Great Britain by True North Books Limited

England HX3 6SN

01422 244555

www.truenorthbooks.com

Printed and Bound by Short Run Press Ltd, Exeter.

*The publishers would like to thank the following companies
for their support in the production of this book*

Peter Hird & Sons
"Specialists within the access platform and lifting industry"

ABI (UK) LTD
"Providing holiday homes for leisurely living"

Andrew Marr International
"Navigating the way to success"

Arco
"Experts in safety"

Alan Wood & Partners
"50 years of technical and professional expertise"

Associated British Ports
"Port of Hull"

BAE Systems
"A proud 100 years in the East Riding"

Beverley Building Society
"A strong independent mutual"

Broady Flow Control Ltd
"Innovative and Effective Solutions"

Burstalls Solicitors
"Professional Legal Services"

Dunston Ship Repairs
"A proud heritage and exciting future"

Europa Crown Ltd
"A world leader in oilseed processing equipment"

E.W. Brown & Son Ltd
"Family-run funeral directors since 1903"

Greens the Signmakers Ltd
"Excellent relationships with clients"

Hull Cartridge Company
"Unrivalled experience in cartridge design and production"

Hymers College
"Educational centre of excellence"

InterTech
"25 years of showcasing their skills"

Neill & Brown Global Logistics
"100 years on the clock and still motoring along"

Smith & Nephew
"Hull roots spread worldwide"

Spencer Group British Engineering
"A home-grown success story"

INTRODUCTION

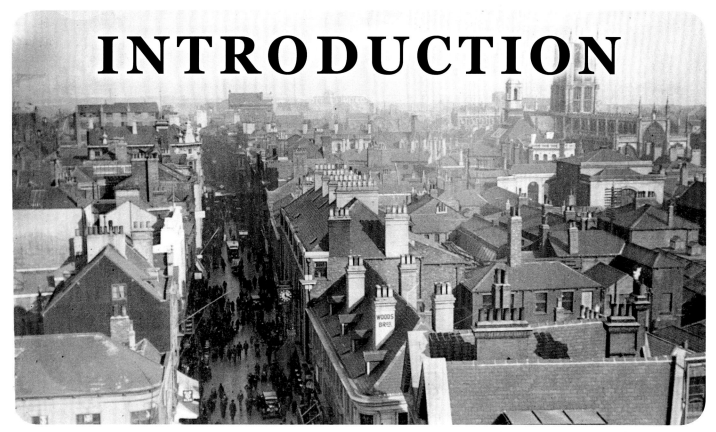

For all of us, memories are the currency which we use to record the changes and progress in our everyday lives and to fix our place as individuals in the greater scheme of things. The is the latest publication in our 'Memories' series of publications, covering nostalgic reflections of towns and cities throughout the UK. In this new book we will be meandering through a pictorial cross-section of life in Kingston upon Hull over the last 100 years or so, to help satisfy the longing we all get from time to time, to recall memories of a different era that now seems better or simpler.

As we get older it is often easier to take a step back, and to view events and developments with a clearer sense of prospective. Our aim has been to assist in this respect by presenting a publication relevant to the area capable of rekindling memories of days gone by in an entertaining and informative manner. Looking through the pages of this book it is interesting to reflect on exactly how much change has taken place in the area over a short period, relative to its long history. Many of these photographs are unique and will inevitably remind us of experiences and events in our lives, of our families and of those whose influence and support has touched us to a greater or lesser degree.

In 2017, Hull became the UK's City of Culture and this will further enhance the city's image and reputation.

There is a definite link between the arts and business and in this publication we have collaborated with a number of the areas most successful businesses to bring you their stories. These companies are here for the long haul and have touched the lives of many Hullensians over the decades.

We can all remember events surrounding friends and family, holidays, weddings, special occasions and nights out in Hull. So let your mind wander and think of the youthful days at the dance hall or courting in one of the many cinemas in the city. Be entertained as we take you on a sentimental journey through the pages of Nostalgic Memories of Kingston upon Hull... Happy Memories!

TEXT	TONY LAX, BRENDAN O'NEILL
PHOTOGRAPHS	BRENDAN O'NEILL
DESIGNER	CHRIS THORPE
BUSINESS DEVELOPMENT MANAGER	PETER PREST
COMPANY PROFILES	BRIAN COATES

CONTENTS

VICTORIAN AND EDWARDIAN HULL

P ublic welfare had become an important factor in the early 1900s not only to politicians but also to local philanthropists who wanted to return some of their wealth to the local people who had helped make them so prosperous. Here we see the building housing the Public Library and Baths on Holderness Rd in 1904. If you stand in front of the building today, to the left you will see the East Hull Pools sign and to the right carved in stone is the name of James Reckitt and the date 1889. James Reckitt, born in 1833 was heir to the household products company Reckitt & Sons along with his two brothers which went on to great success with its products, becoming a public company in 1899 with a reported value of £1.7m, some £562m at today's value! Given this level of wealth, James had several other philanthropic projects including the Garden Village in Hull, a hospital in Withernsea and an orphan's home. The building still stands proudly on Holderness Road today although the adjacent house and shop next door have long since gone.

H ere we have two quite different scenes of Spring Bank in Hull in 1904. In the first we see a broad tree-lined thoroughfare with a chap and his handcart meandering past a very large shire horse just beneath the gas lamp on the right and a number of pedestrians all walking in the same direction on the left hand side, with two trams in the distance. The other photo which could well be from the other direction and taken in the same year shows two trams either side of the central tree lined reservation, with people boarding the one on the left. The building on the right could be the Polar Bear Tavern which was rebuilt in 1895 and later modified in 1911. The chap on his bike may be heading in that direction. Both photos provide a very early view of one of Hull's main arteries

Right: This scene remains central to Hull today as it converges what is now Paragon Street, with King Edward Street and Saville Street. The horse drawn omnibus pulled by two white horses takes centre stage in front of the Lord Londesborough Hotel, whilst the chap with his handcart pushes along his fruit and veg. The gents to the right who look well in their waistcoats and bowler hats may be taking a lunch break on this sunny day around 1904 as many people today would be doing, in what is now an extended pedestrian precinct around the central statue to queen Victoria.

Above: Vane Street today is unrecognisable from this early 1900s photo, it is even difficult to determine whether the street width is the same as the old Vane Street seen here looks quite a wide thoroughfare. This shot is possibly heading away from Spring Bank towards Trafalgar St and these chaps seem to have paused for the photographer. The bearded chap on the right with the bowler hat holds on to his donkey and cart, whilst the refuse collector to the left with his large bin cart maybe just waiting for a house wife to bring out her rubbish for the week. It's a sunny day and by the minimal shadows being cast must be around midday. It would have been a typical scene in Hull around 1904 and looks rather sedate and calm.

This was indeed the beginning of a new era for communications in Britain and Hull was at its forefront. As one of only six authorities to operate their own telephone system in the late 1800s and we see in the fist photo a switchboard operator outside the old Kirkella Exchange in Hull. The boys in the next photo were initially preferred in the role of 'operator' as they had to pass messages orally from one subscriber to the next. Later young girls were chosen for this role, no doubt due to the mischievous nature of the boys in such an important role. As equipment moved forward larger 'switch rooms' were installed and we see in the photo many of the female operators busy in a Hull switch room in 1899. By 1911, all communications of this type, except for the Hull Telephone Department had come under the Post Master General. It

wasn't until the early 1920s that Kingston Communications installed its first Strowger exchange which reduced the need for operator switching of calls. Kingston Com-munications remained a unique part of the communications landscape in Britain for many years to come and was always set apart by its white phone boxes.

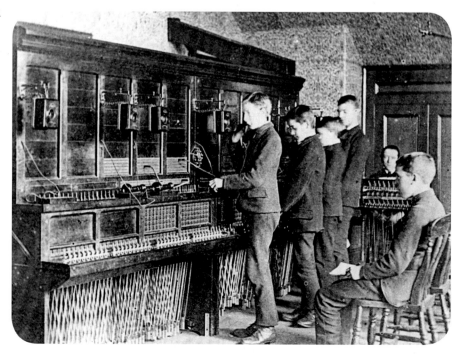

Above: This scene could well have been captured on a quiet Sunday around 1905, with locals wandering serenely across Market Place in Hull. The gent in the foreground, hands clasped behind his back, glances at the young chap just leaving the pavement, whilst the 'old timers' sit around the base of the monument chatting about current affairs which could have included the first public protests by the suffragettes led by Emily Pankhurst or the first £1000 football transfer of Alf Common to Middlesbrough FC. The other two figures conversing in this scene just in front of the Cross Keys Hotel are the 'bobby' and a chap with his thumbs tucked into his waste coat and you can just imagine these two characters passing the time of day. It would be a totally different scene today with new offices dominating both sides of the street.

Left: Here we see a tram making its way along Princes Avenue just passing the junction with Westbourne Avenue, around 1910. A small collection of folk are just about to board the tram whilst the group of young girls may have had a nice morning playing in Pearson Park just off to the right. Apart from the modes of transport, little has changed over the past 100 years with the fine houses on the left still looking very grand with large trees standing proud at each side of the avenue. It is comforting to see that the rigours of war, commercialisation and urban planning have at least left some places untouched.

Monument Bridge or more specifically, the Whitefriargate Lock bridge can be seen in this early photo from around 1910. The title of Monument Bridge was used as the imposing Wilberforce Monument erected in 1834 was originally located at one end of the bridge. Due to growing traffic problems in the area an impressive effort was undertaken in 1935 to relocate 102 foot Doric column to Wilberforce Drive in front of Hull College, where its stands proudly today. The bridge was a main thoroughfare through the city, connecting Queens Dock with Princes Dock in the city centre and was always a very bustling scene as we can see here. There is no motorised transport to be seen but the tram lines give away the progress of transport systems coming to the city. Three chaps on cycles make their way across the bridge, whilst most pedestrians pass in the other direction. To the right of the picture we can see the gas lamp being maintained as a chap sets up his high wooden treadle ladders to reach the glass cage in top. It is clearly a different scene today, although the main buildings in shot remain.

The Hull Fair, as many people know, has been a long standing event for several hundred years and continues to this day. At the turn of the last century it continued to provided entertainment and a brief respite form the drudgery of hard working lives, through the many shows which made up the event, including menageries, American Circus acts, Cinematograph and boxing booths. With the rise in mechanical innovations, roundabouts, boat swings and carousels began to capture the imagination and as we see here, around 1910, the crowds thronged to these events to take part in the fun and see the curiosities featured. Over previous decades, local fairs had gained a bad reputation for rowdiness and

drunkenness, causing many local authorities to withdraw licences and closing fairs down. The Hull fair however continues and no doubt the photo of the Ambulance Station and nurses, shows some moves towards greater control and responsibility and as the sign suggests, a meeting point to find a lost child.

Right: A fine gathering of local Hull folk outside the Builders Hotel in Cogan Street in 1928, shows what must be the landlord and landlady in the doorway with aprons tied around their waists. It is a mixed gathering with mothers holding their babies, a gent in 'plus-fours' and the remainder sporting flat caps, the required headgear of the time. The pub was opened around 1817 and this gathering could well have been celebrating the completion of the re-building of the pub in 1928. Sadly the pub was demolished in the mid 1960s and there is no sign of its existence now in Cogan Street, with its modern flats and offices.

Below: The lack of traffic confirms this early photo of Victoria Square, Hull to be around the turn of the last century. Indeed we can see just the two trams in the foreground and a chap pulling a hand cart, to the right of the tram. Queen Victoria, surveys the scene from her very prominent position overlooking the pedestrians and passers-by, whilst facing the most prominent building in the scene, Hull's Maritime Museum

HULL'S DEEP SEA TRAWLERS

T he depth and scale of Hull's history of deep sea fishing is truly immense. As the worlds largest fishing port in 1960s, the extent and range of the subject requires it to be condensed into 'extracts' which hopefully provide a sense and feeling of what was endured in the deep sea fishing industry for those who worked in it and their families who worried for their safety and return. This short extract will hopefully provide some of that context.

This is an early photograph of a typical trawler company's premises in Hull. Hudson Brothers Trawlers Ltd provided the shipbuilding and repair skills needed to keep trawlers safely on the wild open seas of the North Atlantic and Arctic oceans. The company operated from 1929 to 1969, although it is said to have been founded in 1913 by Tom Hudson who came to Hull from Greenwich. The company was able to distinguish its trawlers by using the name 'Cape' until it was absorbed by the Ross Group in the 1960s. Of course not all shipbuilding premises would be decked with flowers and Union Jacks, but this could well have been in celebration of the Queens coronation in 1953.

Above: Maintenance of trawlers was always a necessary evil, as they would not be earning money if not out trawling for fish. This photo from around 1947 shows 3 steam trawlers held in St Andrews dry dock for repairs. The centre ship is the S.T James Barrie (H460) launched in 1928 in Selby, and requisitioned by the admiralty during the war years 1940-45. The S.T. Welsbach (H277) on the left and a similar steam trawler H399 on the right which was possibly named the Junella and built in Beverley, are seen undergoing their own routine maintenance. These locally built and maintained trawlers provided much needed work for not just the people of Hull, but the many subsidiary companies across the north of England.

ere we see three 'Stern Trawlers' each with its own unique start in life and history behind its voayages which can only be touched upon here. Hulls first stern trawler, the Lord Nelson (H330) arrived from its shipyard in Germany in June 1961.

The first photograph we see here is the Arctic Corsair (H320) built in 1971 in Norway, it later transferred to fishing in the Indian Ocean. The second ship is the Arctic Raider (H440) which was launched on 31st July 1968 and also owned by the Boyd Line. It was a vessel of some notoriety as it was the last ship to leave St Andrews Dock in Hull, at 04.00hrs on 3rd December 1975, before the dock finally closed. It was later scrapped at Gadani Beach in Pakistan, the worlds largest ship breaking yard.

The third photograph is of the Kingston Peridot (H591) built by Cook Welton & Gemmell and launched in 1948. It was originally owned by Kingston Steam Trawler Co.Ltd of Hull before being taken on in 1966 by Hellyer Bros Ltd. This was one of the trawlers from Hull whose fate was to have an impact on the many family and friends waiting at home. On 26/27th January 1968, the vessel had been fishing in heavy seas off Iceland in force 6 gales which later in the day developed in to force 9 gales and worsening icing conditions. Although many attempts were made to contact her by other ships in the area, nothing more was heard that day and she was not seen again. It is thought that the worsening conditions had caused her to ice-up, become top heavy and roll-over. There were 20 men lost at sea that night from the Kingston Peridot and although described as men, two were only 15 and 16 years old. Only the cook from the original crew was left as he had been put ashore in Iceland on 14 Jan after falling on board and suffering neck and chest injuries.

The winter had taken the lives of 58 Hull trawler men with other ships succumbing to the freezing hurricane conditions. The two other ships were the St Romanus which went down on 11th January and the Ross Cleveland on the 5th February that year. The impact of this on the people of Hull was huge and led to the development of support funding for the wives and families of trawler men lost at sea.

Below: The last ship we see is the Stella Polaris (H575) leaving St Andrews dock in the late 1950s. Quite a crowd has gathered to see the ships leave and with a few smart cars parked on the quay, there could even have been dignitaries present. This fine vessel, built by Cook Welton & Gemmell and launched in 1948 had a relatively short life as it was sold for scrap in 1968 and broken up at Ghent that year.

Right: A company based at St Andrews Docks, 'Russell Services' provided communication services for husbands and wives to keep in touch by means of a 'wire' service. As these communications were charged by the word and a word consisted of 5 letters or more, an elaborate code book was provided whereby husband and wife could devise their own, secret code, using just 2 letters for a phrase such as CP meaning 'aboard the ship' and MP meaning 'all is well here' and so on. On a more personal note a husband and wife may have agreed that W would mean 'missing you my darling'. These messages would provide some comfort to those at home, particularly through the harsh winter storms at sea.

This Code Book saves you Money!
Better still, why not use the
'RUSSELL SERVICES'
and save a great deal more?

★

CREWS WIRES
GREETINGS FOR ALL AND EVERY OCCASION
FLOWER SERVICE for
Birthdays, Weddings, Mothering Sunday
or any other purpose
Also Presents of Chocolates, Poultry, etc., etc.

★

Full use of these Services can save you many Pounds

★

Call and arrange your requirements at
RUSSELL SERVICES, LTD.,
66, ST. ANDREW'S DOCK CHAMBERS,
ST. ANDREW'S DOCK, HULL
Telephones: 38157 and 37864

N O T I C E.

THIS CODE BOOK has been compiled to meet the requirements of Fishermen and Short Voyage Seamen.

This Code can be made secret to the persons operating it.

Words that are not in this Code can be made up from the Spelling Table.

Code messages are cheaper, and compact as well as being secret.

The dockside was always a hive of activity when the trawlers came in and it was very much a manual task to haul the fish into baskets and bins or kits and load them over to the waiting 'bobbers' who would label and ice them ready for auction. These wooden, or later aluminium, kits could include, cod, codlings, haddock, skate, coalfish and bergylts and may amount to £11,500 around 1962 for a good catch. But lets not forget, these trawler men had been at sea for around 23 days and would be out again in a couple of days. It didn't leave much after settlings (food, bond, clothing etc) to pass over for housekeeping and a wife who would have looked after the children during the long absences of their father.

Life on board a deep sea trawler was hard and hazardous and that was if the weather stayed fair, which it rarely did in the North Sea. The task to be performed included, 'squaring up the deck, putting up lifelines and manropes, fixing trawls and clearing the fish room, all of this in preparation for the main fishing events. Food was prepared by the cook and bond or duty free cigarettes were issued by the skipper.

The crew were totally occupied once the main trawl had started, hauling and 'shooting' the gear, gutting and heading (if needed) the fish and washing them by hand. This wasn't the end of it as the fish had to be then stowed in the fish room and packed in ice.

It was only when the holds were full of the gleaming silvery fish that they could then head home and rest a little on the way before the ship had to be cleaned. The trawler had to be mopped and cleaned from top to bottom, with any grease on hand rails and portholes being cleared to leave a polished brass shine. Engine rooms were always the pride of the ships chief engineer and his charges would be required to clean this and the footplates to a high shine.

Living together for several weeks on end wasn't easy in a confined place in difficult conditions, but the crews found their ways to enjoy the life and camaraderie was strong on board a Hull Trawler. At times the stormy seas would put lives at risk and the conditions on board in full black oilskins always meant an accident was just around the corner, relying on your mates was a necessity to ensure everyone arrived home safely.

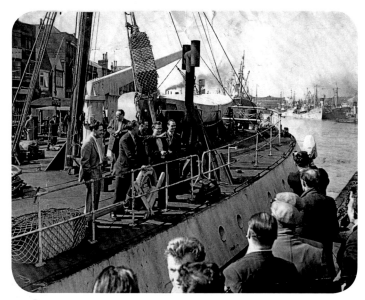

It was a tough life as a trawler man and for their families too as they spent little time at home between trips and were no doubt exhausted when they returned. Their wives and families would have coped in their absence but bringing up children and looking after the house would be no easy task in the 1950s and 60s. Once home the father may have taken their sons to the docks to show them just where dad worked as we see in the photo of the Cape Trafalgar, or their families would wave them off at St Andrews dock on that very same ship. As a reminder in the family home that dad was working hard on the 'high seas', a photograph of the ship, again the Cape Trafalgar, with inserts of mum and dad, would be hung on the wall of the small living room.

Right: After a day and a night at home it would be back to the trawler with goodbyes said at home, as it was considered as very bad luck for families, particularly women, to be seen at the fish dock. The chap we see here, climbing aboard his trawler, was Stan Fenton, the cook for this trip and it is unusual that he is carrying a suitcase as generally only kit bags were allowed on board. Maybe he had his whites and cotton table cloths in there for a special celebration, but probably not, more likely its full of tea towels!

Above: When at home there would be time for some fun at least and the clubs and bars would be the place for the trawler men and their wives to enjoy their short time together, before the men returned to their nominated ship. Many families lived in the Hessle Road area of Hull and the social clubs would provide the haven, at least for a weekend for husbands and wives to enjoy time with their friends.

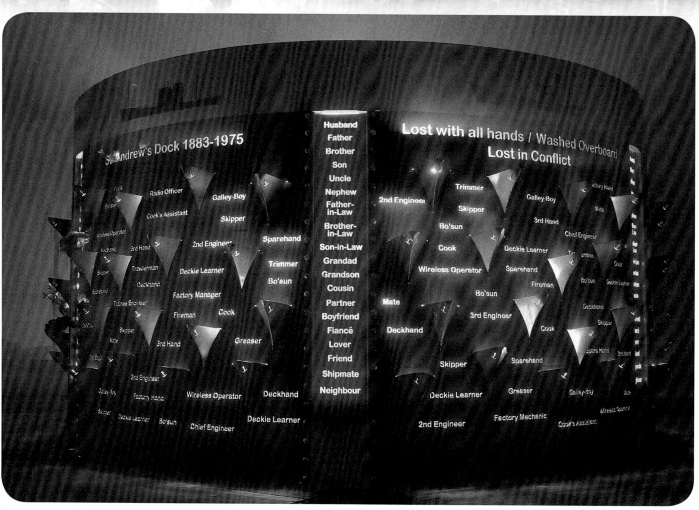

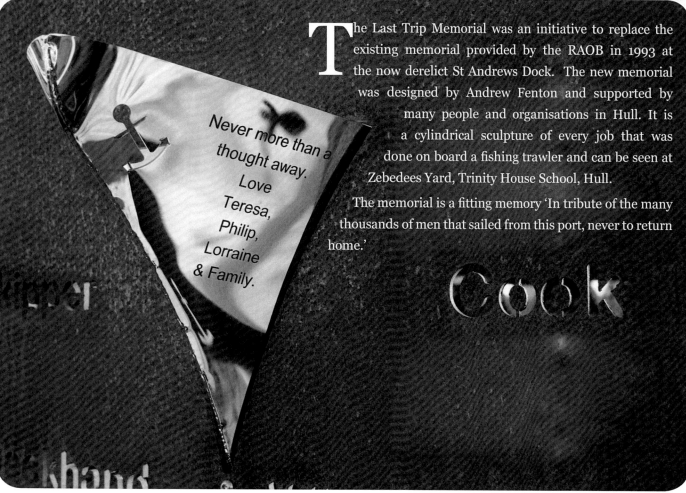

The Last Trip Memorial was an initiative to replace the existing memorial provided by the RAOB in 1993 at the now derelict St Andrews Dock. The new memorial was designed by Andrew Fenton and supported by many people and organisations in Hull. It is a cylindrical sculpture of every job that was done on board a fishing trawler and can be seen at Zebedees Yard, Trinity House School, Hull.

The memorial is a fitting memory 'In tribute of the many thousands of men that sailed from this port, never to return home.'

Never more than a thought away.
Love
Teresa,
Philip,
Lorraine
& Family.

THEATRES & CINEMAS

The Victoria County History records that a theatre is said to have existed in Hull's Whitefriargate at the end of the 16th Century, but no contemporary references to it have been found. Hull City records can identify a company of strolling players visiting the city as far back as 1599 and, earlier still, Hull (like many other towns) had performances of the religious plays from which theatrical tradition was to emerge. The Theatre Royal, Finkle Street, was the first Hull theatre with a known date of construction, having been built in 1768, by the actor-manager Tate Wilkinson.

Hull also embraced the new age of public entertainment. Luxurious cinemas, taking their inspiration from theatres and music halls, were built to accommodate audiences in almost every neighbourhood in the city. For many years Hull had a reputation as being a cinema city. As well as showing the latest films, some venues also featured space for musicians and organs to provide pre-show entertainment. The first purpose-built cinema in Kingston upon Hull was the Prince's Hall which was opened in George Street in 1910 (renamed the Curzon 1955). This form of entertainment became popular and, by 1914, there were 29 cinemas and halls showing films in the city.

Above: The photographer must have been standing in the middle of the road to capture this photograph of the Tivoli Theatre in 1953. Originally the Theatre Royal, the building was adapted and became the Tivoli in 1912. On the bill at that time were Bob and Alf Pearson, a British male vocal duo, who achieved their greatest popularity as an act on the variety stage. The theatre was on the corner of Paragon Street and South Street, with the Imperial Hotel (now Portland Hotel) on one side and the Louisville Pet Shop across the road, just visible on the right of the picture. The old Austin A40 Somerset outside the shop, was actually brand new at the time and was only in production between 1952 and 1954. The Tivoli Theatre closed as a variety theatre in 1954 and was for a short time used as a cinema, prior to being demolished in 1959. Just prior to its closure Arthur Lucan the famous Music Hall and Variety star whose best known character was Old Mother Riley died while backstage. There is a bronze memorial bust of Lucan, which was unveilled on the 8 August, 1986, by Danny La Rue, situated near the spot where he died, in the back of the café in Tivoli House.

Right: Situated in the suburbs at the junction of Holderness Road and Lake Drive, the Astoria Cinema opened on July 30, 1934. It was designed by architect James E. Adamson of London and Hull and constructed by Messrs Markwell, Holmes and Hayter Ltd. In 1935 it was taken over by the County Cinemas circuit, but returned to a independent operator a year later. It closed after 29 years on 7 June, 1963, and immediately reopened as the Astoria Bingo Club – well over 45

years on this continues successfully. The Astoria Cinema is largely unaltered inside, very attractive, and is extremely well maintained.

Below: Located in the north of Hull. The Monica Picture House was opened on 26 November, 1914. Around the time of this photograph the cinema was equipped with CinemaScope. We can date this picture fairly accurately to 1955, when 'The Ladykillers', starring Alec Guinness and Peter Sellers first appeared on the big screen. The Monica Picture House was closed in October 1960. It was converted into The Piper Club, which still operates today and is popular with the many young students who live in the area. The original white stone façade has now been replaced with a modern fascia and the former foyer is now an open courtyard which leads to the entrance of the auditorium.

Right: Located on the corner of George Street and Bourne Street, the Alexandra Theatre opened on 26 December, 1902, with a production of the play "A Royal Divorce". Designed in a Renaissance style by architect William Guest, a feature of its exterior was a large tower on the Bourne Street corner. Inside the auditorium seating was provided in orchestra stalls, pit stalls, dress circle, balcony and gallery levels. By the early-1930's it was presenting variety shows. The Alexandra was destroyed by German bombs in 1941. Housing has since been built on the site.

Cinema as a form of entertainment became popular and, by 1914, there were 29 cinemas and halls showing films in the city. Hull embraced the new age of public entertainment. Luxurious cinemas, taking their inspiration from theatres and music halls, were built to accommodate audiences in almost every neighbourhood in the city.

In the east of Hull there were three cinemas on George Street; the Dorchester, the Curzon and the Criterion. The very first purpose-built cinema in Kingston upon Hull was the Prince's Hall

which was opened in George Street to an eager Hull public in 1910. It was located directly across from the Grand Opera House. In the mid-1950s it was re-named Curzon Cinema, but was subsequently closed in February 1960. At one point it was converted into a club. It was demolished around 1985.

In 1968, both British and American drama films were on the screen at the Criterion Picture Theatre, where Malcolm McDowell in "If" and Steve McQueen in "Bullitt" were the leading men on show.

These two photographs (left and below) were taken probably 60 years apart and despite changes to the external facade, you can still see it is the same building. Designed by noted theatre architect Frank Matcham it was opened as the Grand Opera House on 9 January, 1893, but despite the name it was used for drama productions. In 1930 it was remodeled and films were now shown instead of stage plays. The change was successful so in July 1935 the theatre was closed for three months for extensive renovations by architects Blackmore & Sykes. The front of the old theatre was also modernised but much of the original facade can still be identified from these images. The Dorchester Cinema opened on 30 December, 1935 with Will Hay in "Boys Will Be Boys". Now operated by Associated Hull Cinemas Ltd, The Dorchester Cinema showed first run movies for many years and later was also home to many long run epics such as "South Pacific" and "Ben-Hur". It was closed in 1977 because of declining audiences and demolished in 1987. The site is now occupied by a bar and store complex.

Left: The writing was on the wall, however, for the Criterion which was to close a few months later in June 1969. The cinema was originally opened as the Majestic on 1 February, 1915. It was closed in the summer of 1935 for renovations to be carried out to be carried out and re-opened as the Criterion Picture Theatre. In 1950 the Criterion was owned by Associated Hull Cinemas Ltd. A notable feature were the two stone lions which guarded its entrance. When the building was to be demolished the two stone lions were rescued and are now situated in Hornsea Memorial Gardens.

Below: A lone policeman stands in the middle of the road as theatregoers leave the New Theatre in Hull. The photograph was taken in April 1954 looking across Kingston Square. The large crowd had just watched a performance of 'And So To Bed', a musical adaptation of a play by J.B. Fagan about the English diarist, Samuel Pepys. Throughout its life, the Hull New Theatre has faced challenges and uncertainty, yet it has remained true to the purpose for which it was intended. Born out of one man's dream, Peppino Santangelo, to create a tradition of 'playing for the people', Hull New Theatre first opened in a blaze of glory in 1939, as a successor to the Hull Repertory Theatre Company. Despite a direct hit in World War Two, the theatre is still going strong today. The theatre, now a Grade II listed building, closed on 4 January, 2016, for a major refit in preparation of Hull being the UK City of Culture.

Above: A wonderfully ornate Edwardian cinema surviving – but only just – into the 21st Century. Opened on June 1, 1914. It was designed by H. Percival Binks and seated 1,200 in the stalls and single balcony. Above this is parapet with a bare breasted female figure perched on top looking down into Anlaby Road. At first there was an 'excellent' orchestra who played in a box at the side of the screen. Sound equipment was introduced in 1929. In September 1978 the Tower Cinema closed as a full time cinema and was restored to near pristine condition as a music and boxing venue – although films were also occasionally presented by the Hull Film Society. This was short lived however and in 1983 it became a nightclub and fun pub – both of which uses took their toll of the interior. After being closed for a number of years, the Tower was refurbished in 2003 and became another nightclub in the town. The Tower Cinema is a Grade II Listed building.

Left: The Palace Theatre of Varieties, in Anlaby Road, opened on 6 December, 1897 and was run by the Liverpool, Leeds, and Hull Empire Company. At the time, it was considered to be a beautiful theatre and a great acquisition to the town. It was designed and erected under the personal supervision of the renowned theatre architect, Mr Frank Matcham. The Theatre remained in variety use until it was damaged by bombing during the war in 1940. It then remained closed for the next 10 years until it was eventually leased to Kingston Varieties who also owned the Tivoli Theatre in Hull at the time. They repaired and reopened the Palace Theatre in 1951, and then both Theatres ran in unison for a short time, until the Tivoli was turned into a Continental Cinema in 1954. Later the Palace Theatre operated for several years as a nightspot called the Hull Continental Palace Theatre. Even this ended in July 1965 however and the Theatre was demolished the following year.

Below: At the time of this photograph in December 1957, this was a very unique way of advertising. The innovative idea was used to promote the latest film at Hull's Cecil Cinema. The unusual electric delivery vehicles were used by British Railways and made local deliveries from Paragon Station. They were advanced for their time, being almost silent in operation, and significantly, fume-free as they scurried around the city streets. The film being advertised was 'Robbery Under Arms', starring Peter Finch, Ronald Lewis, Maureen Swanson and a youthful David McCallum (later to be known for his role as mysterious Russian agent Illya Kuryakin, in the Man from U.N.C.L.E.

Only older readers will recognise this view of the derelict Cecil Theatre in 1953, prior to demolition. Life was getting back to normal but the ravages of war were still evident. The Cecil Theatre's demise came during bombing on the night of 7/8 May, 1941, when German incendiary bombs reduced the building to a shell; and it remained like that until it was raised to the group shortly after this picture was taken. Originally built as the Theatre De-Luxe in 1911, the building was rebuilt and renamed the Cecil Theatre in 1925. The poster from the opening year, advertised the great Rudolph Valentino in the film, Monsieur Beaucaire, only two years before his untimely death. It is also promoting 'the most luxurious café in the city'. The Cecil Cinema (last operated as the Cannon Cecil Cinema and a Mecca Bingo Club) was built on the site and grounds of a Mariners' Hospital/Almshouses on the opposite corner across from the former Cecil Theatre in shot. The quaint buildings on the right hand side of the image are still in evidence today, at what is now a busy junction of Anlaby Road and Ferensway.

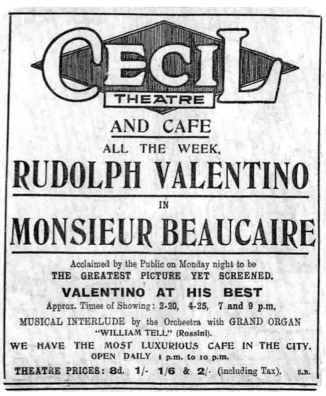

We have used this photograph before in a previous Hull book, but it is such a cheerful and happy scene that we have included it again. The fun -loving young women of the Tivoli Theatre chorus line can be seen posing for a photograph in the King George Dock area in 1951. The two lucky men in the picture are providing support for the ladies, in more ways than one, and probably acting as chaperones. Entertainment during and years after the Second World War provided civilians with a form of escape from the hardships of wartime life in Britain. It was still very risque in the early 1950s to see a glimpse of stocking tops, particularly in public, so the young lady doing the splits in the front is certainly doing her best to attract an audience to the show. Nylons had started to trickle into shops for ordinary women to buy, but understandably they were expensive. Sadly, the extra benefit from such promotions was short lived, as the Tivoli closed as a variety theatre, only three years after this photograph was taken.

People pour out of Mayfair Bingo Club in Beverley Road on 16 March, 1965, shortly after it had opened as a Bingo Hall. Located in a popular area of Hull, the Mayfair Cinema pictured right, was opened on 7 October, 1929. It was designed by architect H.F. Wharf, and had seating provided in stalls and circle levels. It also had a café attached for the convenience of its patrons. It closed as a cinema around the time of the time of the picture from 1964, in which we can see the latest Elvis Presley movie 'Kissin' Cousins' was being advertised. The independently operated Mayfair Casino Bingo Club was later taken over by Mecca Bingo Clubs chain. In 1998, it was converted into a public house called the Hogshead and later it became Hollywood & Vine.

FAMOUS PEOPLE FROM HULL

Some of the people you might not realise have links with Hull

Hull and the surrounding areas have entertained a multitude of famous people. A selection of those who were born in the Hull area, or have lived within the borders of the borough are...

William Wilberforce (right) was an English politician, philanthropist, and a leader of the movement to eradicate the slave trade, born 24 August, 1759. A native of Hull, he began his political career in 1780, eventually becoming an independent Member of Parliament (MP) for Yorkshire (1784–1812). In 1785, he became an Evangelical Christian, which resulted in major changes to his lifestyle and a lifelong concern for reform. In later years, Wilberforce supported the campaign for the complete abolition of slavery. In Hull a public subscription in 1834 funded the Wilberforce Monument, a 31-metre (102 ft) Greek Doric column topped by a statue of Wilberforce, which now stands in the grounds of Hull College near Queen's Gardens. Wilberforce's birthplace was acquired by the city corporation in 1903 and, following renovation, Wilberforce House in Hull was opened as Britain's first slavery museum.

John Venn, FRS, (below) was an English logician and philosopher noted for introducing the Venn diagram, used in the fields of set theory, probability, logic, statistics, and computer science. Venn was born on 4 August, 1834 in Kingston to Martha Sykes and Rev. Henry Venn, who was the rector of the parish of Drypool. In 1866, Venn published The Logic of Chance, a groundbreaking book that espoused the frequency theory of probability, offering that probability should be determined by how often something is forecast to occur as opposed to "educated" assumptions. Venn then further developed mathematician George Boole's theories in the 1881 work Symbolic Logic, in which he highlighted what would become known as Venn diagrams. Venn is

commemorated at the University of Hull by the Venn Building, built in 1928. He died on 4 April, 1923.

Britain's richest ever businessman lived a much more low profile existence than modern business billionaires like, Richard Branson, Bill Gates and Roman Abramovich, who are household names. **John Ellerman** was born on Anlaby Road, Hull in 1862. He was the son of a German corn merchant who had come to the city from Hamburg in 1850. His father died when John was 9 years old and left him a legacy of £600. After passing his exams he moved to London and set up his own accountancy practice. Ellerman began with shipping lines, but diversified into brewing, newspapers (he was a major shareholder of The Times and the Daily Mail), coalmining and property, owning swathes of prime residential areas in central London. He was awarded a baronetcy in 1905, for his support in providing the government with ships during the Boer War. In 1916 Ellerman acquired the Hull based Wilson Line, once the world's largest privately owned fleet. Despite his vast wealth he lived a quiet, low-profile existence away from high society. The secretive tycoon from Hull died in 1933 and left the largest estate in probate history.

Admiral Henry Wolsey Bayfield (right) was a British naval officer and surveyor. Bayfield was born in Kingston-upon-Hull in 1795. He joined the Royal Navy on 6 January, 1806 at the age of 10, as a volunteer on HMS Pompee. He was commissioned as a lieutenant on 20 March 1815, and in the summer of 1816 assisted Captain William Fitzwilliam Owen in surveying various Canadian rivers and lakes. In June 1817, Bayfield was made the admiralty surveyor for North America. He was promoted commander in 1826, and the following year, he travelled to Quebec to complete surveys of the St Lawrence River. He retired on 31 March, 1866, and was promoted admiral on the retired list in 1867. The town of Bayfield, Ontario, the cities of Bayfield, Nova Scotia and Bayfield, Wisconsin are named after him. He died in Charlottetown on 10 February, 1885, at the age of 90.

Patricia Bredin (born 1935) (right) is a British actress and one-time singer from Hull, who was best known as the very first United Kingdom representative in the Eurovision Song Contest. She took part in the 1957 contest, held in Frankfurt, and finished in seventh place out of ten entries with the song "All", the first ever song sung in English at the Eurovision. According to The Eurovision Song Contest - The Official History by John Kennedy O'Connor at 1:52, this is the shortest performance in the history of the contest. Patti as she was known scored 6 points, with the winning song from the Netherlands receiving 31 points. In 1962, Bredin had the distinction of succeeding Julie Andrews as Guenevere in the Broadway production of Camelot. In 1964, she married singer Ivor Emmanuel, but they had no children, and divorced within two years. On her second marriage, she married the Canadian businessman Charles MacCulloch and became Patricia Bredin-McCulloch, but tragically he died on their honeymoon.

Sir John Hall was born in Hull in 1924, the third son of George Hall, a captain in the navy. At the age of ten he was sent to school in Switzerland and his education continued in Paris and Hamburg. After returning to England and being employed by the Post Office, at the age of 27 he decided to emigrate. Hall emigrated to New Zealand, on the Samarang, arriving in Lyttelton on 31 July, 1852. His brothers George and Thomas followed him to New Zealand soon after. He developed one of the first large scale sheep farming runs in Canterbury. On 8 October 1879, he was appointed the Premier of New Zealand. Despite the distances involved, Hall married Rose Dryden in England, daughter of William Dryden of Kingston upon Hull, after returning there in 1860. They went back to New Zealand in 1863. Knighted in 1882, he continued to sit in the House from 1887, and his last public act was to successfully pilot the bill granting women's suffrage through the House. Sir John retired from politics in 1893 but was honoured by his province by being elected mayor of Christchurch in 1906 for its international exhibition. Hall died in Christchurch the following year, shortly after the exhibition had finished.

Florence Margaret Smith was born in Hull on the 20 September, 1902. The second daughter of Ethel Rachel Spear and Charles Ward Smith, she was called "Peggy" within her family, but acquired the nickname "Stevie" as a young woman. The first work by Stevie Smith to be published was a collection of six poems, which appeared in the New Statesman in 1935. Her style was often very dark; her characters were perpetually saying "goodbye" to their friends or welcoming death. Later that year, she submitted further poems to the publisher Chatto and Windus but was advised to 'go away and write a novel'. This she did, writing at home and in her office, using the yellow paper used at Newnes Publishing Company for carbon copies. Novel on Yellow Paper or Work It Out For Yourself was published in 1936 (by Jonathan Cape rather than Chatto and Windus) and was an instant success. Her first volume of poetry, A Good Time Was Had By All, was published in 1937. Following the publication of her best known collection Not Waving But Drowning in 1957 she became more widely known and throughout the 1960s was increasingly popular in Britain and America.

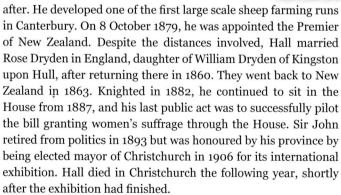

Joseph Patrick Longthorne MBE (Left) was born into a show business family, his parents both being travelling show people. He is from Hessle Road, Hull, known for its fishing community, thus considers himself as a "Hessle Roader." He attended Villa Place Primary School and Sydney Smith High School. When he was six, he came first in a talent show and his prize was a toy motor car. At fourteen he landed a part in Yorkshire Television's series Junior Showtime, and remained with the show for over two years. He then turned professional and earned a living in Northern working men's clubs. It was through the London Weekend Television series Search For a Star in 1981, that Longthorne was first launched onto the British televiewing public as a singer and impressionist. In 2007 the Variety Club awarded him their Lifetime Achievement Award, which placed him amongst past recipients such as Frank Sinatra, Judy Garland, and Ella Fitzgerald. He was appointed Member of the Order of the British Empire (MBE) in the 2012 Birthday Honours for services to charity.

David Whitfield (below) was a popular British male tenor vocalist from Hull. He became the first British Artist to have a UK No.1 single in his home country and in the United States at the time with "Cara Mia". He died from a brain haemorrhage in Sydney, Australia, while on tour at the age of 54. A statue in the memory of Whitfield was unveiled outside of the New Theatre in Hull on 31 August 2012, before the opening night of a show celebrating his life and music. Whitfield was born in Hull on 2 February, 1925. He sang in the choir at his church during his childhood and entertained his fellow members of the Royal Navy during the Second World War. After the war, he appeared on Opportunity Knocks, a talent show on Radio Luxembourg. Whitfield was the most successful British male singer in America during the 50s . He was the first British male vocalist to earn a gold disc and the third overall. He was the first to reach the Top Ten of the Billboard Top 100, and the first artist from Britain to sell over a million copies of a record in the US.

Sir (William) Alfred Gelder born on 12 May, 1855 was a British architect and Liberal politician. Gelder was born in the village of North Cave, the son of William Gelder, a joiner and wheelwright who later became a timber merchant. In 1877 he married Elizabeth Parker from Hull. Gelder wanted to be an architect and he went to Hull to seek out opportunities. According to one source it was largely thanks to Gelder's ability and energy that Hull was a city transformed – with old buildings removed, new wide streets introduced and attractive shops and public offices erected. Under Gelder's supervision, Hull was being hailed as one of the country's finest cities with the slums and disorder of the Victorian city giving way to broad, straight thoroughfares. During Gelder's time the city centre was reconstructed and a new bridge, the Drypool Bridge, was built across the River Hull. In recognition of Gelder's contributions, the new road built through the city centre to link with this bridge was named Alfred Gelder Street. From 1899-1903 Gelder was Liberal Mayor of Hull and in all was a member of the council, later in the office of Alderman, for 43 years. He was knighted in the King's birthday honours list of 1903 for his services to architecture and to the City of Hull. In 1930 he received the Honorary Freedom of the City.

Philip Arthur Larkin was an English poet, novelist and librarian. His first book of poetry, The North Ship, was published in 1945, followed by two novels, Jill (1946) and A Girl in Winter (1947), and he came to prominence in 1955 with the publication of his second collection of poems. After graduating from Oxford in 1943 with a first in English language and literature, Larkin became a librarian. It was during the thirty years he worked with distinction as university librarian at the Brynmor Jones Library at the University of Hull that he produced the greater part of his published work. One of Larkin's colleagues at Hull said he became a great figure in post-war British librarianship. Ten years after the new library's completion, Larkin computerized records for the entire library stock, making it the first library in Europe to install a GEAC system, an automated online circulation system. In 2010, Larkin's adopted home city, Kingston upon Hull, commemorated him with the Larkin 25 Festival, which culminated in the unveiling of a statue of Larkin by Martin Jennings on 2 December, 2010, the 25th anniversary of his death.

Born in Hull in 1934, **Shirley Craven** studied art at Hull College of Art and then printed textiles at the Royal College of Art, 1955-58. In 1959, aged 25, she started work at Hull Traders, a textiles firm founded two years earlier in Willesden, London, by entrepreneur Tristam Hull. In 1963, she became Chief Designer and a Director of the firm, where she worked for nearly two decades. In 1960 Design magazine described the company as having a 'high reputation for producing adventurous and exciting designs', which they attributed to the tight control of Craven, who displayed a 'dramatic and original handling of colour and pattern'. According to the Textile Society, Craven 'pioneered an aesthetic more akin to painting than textiles', breaking 'all the rules' and 'revolutionising post-war furnishings with her dramatic, unconventional large-scale designs'. Her bold patterns and colours were commercially successful, capturing the style of the swinging sixties and received critical acclaim. She won the Design Centre awards three times.

2016 marked the 75th anniversary of the death of **Amy Johnson,** CBE, Hull's flying heroine was born at 154 St. George's Road, in 1903. She was one of the most influential and inspirational women of the twentieth century. Educated at Boulevard Municipal Secondary School (later Kingston High School) and the University of Sheffield, she was the first woman to fly solo from England to Australia and set a string of other records throughout her career. During the 1920s and 1930s aviation was dominated by the rich and famous and most female pilots were titled women such as Lady Heath, the Duchess of Bedford and Lady Bailey. But Amy was the first woman to gain a ground engineer's "C" licence and, whilst working as a secretary to a solicitor, William Charles Crocker, she took flying lessons. In 1929 she was awarded her pilot's "A" licence and just a year later set of solo for Australia. During the Second World War, Johnson joined the newly formed Air Transport Auxiliary (ATA), whose job was to transport Royal Air Force aircraft around the country. There is still some mystery surrounding the accident that led to Amy's death on 5 January, 1941. While flying an Airspeed Oxford for the ATA from Prestwick to RAF Kidlington near Oxford, Johnson went off course in adverse weather conditions. Reportedly out of fuel, she bailed out as her aircraft crashed into the Thames Estuary. Despite a brave rescue attempt, Johnson's body was never recovered.

John Alderton (right) was born in Gainsborough, Lincolnshire, the son of Ivy (née Handley) and Gordon John Alderton. He grew up in Hull where he attended Kingston High School. Alderton first became familiar to television viewers in 1962, when he played Dr Moone in the ITV soap opera, Emergency – Ward 10. He married his co-star, Jill Browne, but they later divorced. After appearing in British films such as The System (1964), Assignment K (1968), Duffy (1968) and Hannibal Brooks (1969), he played the lead in the comedy series Please Sir!, as hapless teacher Mr Hedges. He later transferred to another top-rated ITV series when he played Thomas Watkins, the chauffeur, in Upstairs, Downstairs, opposite his wife, Pauline Collins. From 1987 to 1994, he narrated and voiced all the characters in the original series of Fireman Sam.

Thomas Robinson Ferens (below) born on 4 May, 1847 was a British politician, a philanthropist, and an industrialist. He was the Member of Parliament for Hull East for 13 years, and served the city as a Justice of the Peace and as High Steward. He helped establish Reckitt & Sons, a manufacturer of household goods, as one of Kingston upon Hull's foremost businesses. In October, 1911, Ferens was presented with the Freedom of the City of Hull. In the following year he was made a member of the Privy Council by King George V and later in the year, he was also made

High Steward of Hull. He became very wealthy but his Methodist up-bringing meant that he used his wealth for the benefit of others. He made gifts to the city totalling over £1m (equivalent to £45m today) funding a variety of causes including the city's art gallery and the formation of Hull University. Following a few weeks of illness, Ferens died on Friday 9th May, 1930. Two funeral services were held at the same time in the city – one at Brunswick Church and the other at Holy Trinity Church. The year after his death, a pageant was held to mark the opening of Ferensway, a major new thoroughfare in the centre of the city. The Times reported that it would "rank as one of the finest in the North of England", and continued, "The street is 100 ft wide, 10 ft wider than Regent Street in London." Although Ferens was not born in Hull, it was his home for over sixty years and it became his 'adopted city'.

John Ward was the outstanding Hull artist of the heyday of marine painting, born in the city in December, 1798, the son of Abraham Ward, master mariner. He has been described as "the leading marine artist and ship portrait painter in Hull during the first half of the 19th century". By 1826, Ward was listed in the local Hull Directory as a "House and Ship Painter". He subsequently produced small watercolour paintings and some larger oil paintings, of local maritime and shipping scenes. He made many engravings of his own works. Sadly his life was to be cut short in 1849; an epidemic of cholera introduced from the continent

which had spread through the major towns along the east coast. However, it was not until 1883 that his importance was recognized when the local press briefly described his life. In 1981 an exhibition of his works was held at the Ferens Art Gallery to coincide with the opening of the Humber Bridge. Today, John Ward of Hull, is recognised as one of the world's greatest marine artists.

Ian Gillett Carmichael, (below) OBE born on Sunnybank and grew up in Westbourne Avenue, West Hull in the 1920s, was an English actor best known for his roles in the films of the Boulting brothers such as Private's Progress (1956) and I'm All Right Jack (1959). Later he played Dorothy L. Sayers's Gentleman Detective, Lord Peter Wimsey, on television and radio. The son of an optician, he was educated at Scarborough College and Bromsgrove School, before training as an actor at RADA. Before the war, the young actor left his family business in Hull to attend the Royal Academy

of Dramatic Arts and to sing in talent contests at the Hammersmith Palais de Danse. In the years which followed his demob from the British Army in 1947, Carmichael worked mostly on stage and continued to act until shortly before he died. In 1999, he appeared in the BBC serial Wives and Daughters. In the ITV series Heartbeat, and its spin-off The Royal. He was appointed an OBE in the 2003 Queen's Birthday Honours List.

Dorothy Mackaill (right) was a British-American actress, born on 4 March, 1903, most notably of the silent-film era and into the early 1930s. Born in Hull, Mackaill lived with her father after her parents separated when she was eleven. She attended Thoresby Primary School. As a teenager she ran away to London to pursue a stage career as an actress. After temporarily relocating to Paris, she met a Broadway stage choreographer who persuaded her to move to New York City where she became involved in the Ziegfeld Follies and befriended future motion picture actresses Marion Davies and Nita Naldi. In 1924, Mackaill rose to leading lady status in the drama The Man Who Came Back, opposite rugged matinee idol George O'Brien. She made a smooth transition to sound with the part-talkie The Barker (1928) and had success in talkies for the next couple of years. Her most memorable role of this era was the 1932 Columbia Pictures release Love Affair with a young Humphrey Bogart as her leading man. She made several films for MGM, Paramount and Columbia before retiring in 1937.

Vanessa Hooper, is a retired English ballerina and theatre dancer who now works as a dance teacher, freelance choreographer, lecturer and examiner. She is the principal of the Skelton-Hooper School of Dance, which was founded by her mother, Vera Skelton. She was born and raised in the city of Hull. At 16, she was contracted to The Royal Ballet based at the Royal Opera House in Covent Garden. She was later contracted to Northern Ballet Theatre, a ballet and theatrical dance company based in Leeds. After the death of her father, she was given leave from the company, but despite her contract being left open, she decided to resign permanently and returned to Hull, becoming a dance teacher working alongside her mother. She later returned to the theatre, making her West End theatre debut in a musical based on the life of Marilyn Monroe. Most recently she has become the resident dance expert for the television series Ladette to Lady.

Gavin Scott was born in 1950 in Hull. He is a writer and producer, known for Small Soldiers, The Borrowers, and writer of the Emmy-winning mini-series The Mists of Avalon (2001). He grew up in Summergangs Road and was a former Cavendish Road pupil, leaving in 1961 for New Zealand, after Duncan, Gavin's father, was made redundant from his job at Waddington's glove factory. At 17 he spent a year as a volunteer teacher in the jungles of Borneo, working with the children of head-hunters, after which he studied history and political science at Victoria University of Wellington, and journalism at the Wellington Polytechnic. He produced and directed more than two hundred documentaries and short films for BBC and the commercial TV in the UK before moving to the United States, where his first assignment was with George Lucas, developing and scripting "The Young Indiana Jones Chronicles". Scott has happy memories of his time as a child in Hull, recalling a time catching tiddlers in the pond at East park and the joke shop in the Hepworth Arcade he visited on his return to England in the 1970s.

Undoubtedly one of the city's pioneers, **J. Arthur Rank** was born in Hull in 1888. He was born into a devoutly Methodist family. His father, Joseph, had founded a flour milling business in 1875, which had started with a rented windmill on Holderness Road. The company prospered and was a substantial business by the time of his death in 1943. Joseph Rank's Flour Mill can still be seen today on the banks of the River Hull next to Drypool Bridge, a testament to a prominent local business. J. Arthur Rank moved into film production as a way of promoting the Christian message. The Rank Organisation grew to dominate British film production in the 1940s and 50s, operating the Odeon cinema chain and building Pinewood Studios. He became Lord Rank in 1957 and set up a charitable foundation before his death in 1973. The home where film producer J Arthur Rank was born (Rank House), in Holderness Road, has been restored after standing derelict for over a decade.

A HULL INDUSTRIALIST WHO BECAME BRITAIN'S CHIEF MAKER AND DISTRIBUTOR OF MOTION PICTURES, **J ARTHUR RANK** WAS BORN HERE ON 22 DECEMBER 1888.

HULL CIVIC SOCIETY

Few people realise that the first ever FA football rule book was devised by a man from Hull. **Ebenezer Cobb Morley** was an English sportsman and is regarded as the father of the Football Association and modern football. He was born in 1831 and lived at 10 Garden Square, Princess Street, in Hull and lived in the city until he was 22. He moved to Barnes in 1858 forming the Barnes Club, a founding member of the FA, in 1862. In 1863, as captain of the Mortlake-based club, he wrote to Bell's Life newspaper proposing a governing body for the sport, that led to the first meeting at the Freemasons' Tavern, that created the FA. He was the FA's first secretary (1863–1866) and its second president (1867–1874) and drafted the first Laws of the Game at his home in Barnes. As a player, he played in the first ever match, against Richmond in 1863, and scored in the first representative match, between the clubs of London and Sheffield on 31 March 1866. It was not all plain sailing as some members objected to some rules as they considered them to be "uncivilised". Others believed that charging, hacking and tripping were important ingredients of the game. Ebenezer Cobb Morley died in 1924.

Alan Frederick Plater was born in Jarrow, although his family moved to Hull in 1938. He attended Kingston High School, where Tom Courtenay became a lifetime friend. Plater was an English playwright and screenwriter, who worked extensively in British television from the 1960s to the 2000s. He wrote 18 episodes of the BBC's pioneering police series Z Cars between 1963 and 1965, and 30 episodes for its sequel, Softly Softly. A regional affinity with the North, even in series produced in London such as Z Cars, was the hallmark of much of his work, together with an appetite for comedy and a gift for writing dialogue. In Hull he started the Spring Street theatre, home to John Godber's Hull Truck company. He was a supporter of Hull City A.F.C.. His play Confessions of a City supporter on his lifelong relationship with the club was staged during the first ever run of performances at the theatre's new home. The new building in the centre of the city is an appropriate testament to him.

Ralph & Gerald Thomas were English film directors born in Hull. Ralph, was perhaps best known for directing the Doctor series of films. His brother, Gerald Thomas, was also a film director, probably best remembered for the Carry On... film series and his son is the Academy Award-winning film producer, Jeremy Thomas. The brothers lived in Westbourne Avenue between 1926 – 1929, and today on the wall of the house is a green plaque to commemorate this fact. Coincidentally, the same West Hull street was also the birthplace of actor Ian Carmichael, who became one of the most bankable British stars of the 1950s.

> RALPH & GERALD THOMAS
> FILM DIRECTORS
> LIVED HERE
> 1926-1929

Gerald's older brother Ralph worked with Peter Rogers' wife Betty Box on the popular Doctor series which Ralph directed. Gerald worked as an editor in the cutting room with Betty but he had ambitions to direct and Peter, then a young producer, backed him. Together they made a formidable team whose skill has combined to create a British Institution in the Carry On films.

Sir Tom Courtenay, (Below) the 77-year-old actor was born in Hull near the city's fish docks and is president of the Hull City official supporters club. He shot to fame in the 1960s in films such as The Loneliness of the Long Distance Runner, Billy Liar and Doctor Zhivago. Courtenay was born in Hull, the son of Annie Eliza (née Quest) and Thomas Henry Courtenay, a boat painter. He attended Kingston High School and studied drama at the Royal Academy of Dramatic Art (RADA) in London. Since the mid-1960s, he has been known primarily for his work in the theatre, although he received an Academy Award nomination for Best Actor for the film adaptation of The Dresser (1983). In

1999, Courtenay (right) was awarded an honorary doctorate by Hull University. In February, 2001, he was knighted by the Queen at Buckingham Palace, in recognition of his 40 years on stage and screen. He recently returned to East Yorkshire to film the big screen adaption of the classic sitcom Dad's Army, playing the role of L/Cpl Jones.

Since making her debut in the film version of Up the Junction in 1968, the Hull-born actress **Maureen Lipman** has enjoyed a remarkably varied career that has seen her appear in hit TV shows such as Jonathan Creek and Doctor Who. She has also starred in films as wildly diverse as Carry on Columbus and Roman Polanski's The Pianist, and was part of the National Theatre during the early 1970s under the charge of Sir Laurence Olivier. Lipman was the daughter of Maurice Julius Lipman and Zelma Pearlman. Her father was a tailor; he used to have a shop between the Ferens Art Gallery and Monument Bridge. She attended Newland School for Girls and became interested in performing as a youth. In recent years she has perhaps become best known for her comic roles and this week she stars in To Hull and Back – a series for BBC Radio 4, which paired her with fellow Hullensian Lucy Beaumont, who wrote the script. In a recent newspaper interview she was quoted as saying, "she's delighted by Hull's rejuvenation in recent years – epitomised by its successful bid to become UK City of Culture in 2017 – but says unless you're from the city you probably don't get what all the fuss is about. If you come from Hull you assume that everyone else gets what's interesting and weird about it".

Ronnie Hilton (right) was one of those 1950s vocalists whose career coincided with rock 'n' roll's 1956 onslaught on the ballad-dominated hit parade, he had nine top 20 hits between 1954 and 1957. Hilton's approach owed much to the "nice 'n' easy" style of Americans such as Bing Crosby, Eddie Fisher and Perry Como. Born Adrian Hill in Hull, Hilton left school at 14 and worked in an aircraft factory in the early days of the second world war before being called up into the Highland Light Infantry. Demobbed in 1947, he became a fitter in a Leeds sewing machine plant. In the evenings he performed with the Johnny Addlestone band at the Starlight Roof in Leeds and it was there that he was heard by HMV's A&R manager, Walter Ridley, who suggested that to be successful he would have to change his name. He started singing professionally under his adopted name in 1954 after leaving his safe job and success followed. He came to fame by supplying smoothly delivered cover versions of popular American songs during the 1950s. Hilton kept on performing well into the 1960s, in summer seasons and Christmas shows, and was also a regular fixture in pantomimes in Hull, at the New Theatre. In 1989 the British Academy of Song Composers and Authors awarded him its gold medal for services to popular music.

Brian Norman Roger Rix, CBE, DL, (below) was a brilliant comedy actor with a career spanning more than three decades. He was born in Cottingham on 27 January 1924, the youngest of four children. His father, Herbert Rix, and Herbert's two brothers, ran the shipping (and subsequently oil) company in Hull, founded by his grandfather Robert Rix. His sister Sheila became an actress during his school days, and Rix himself developed the same ambition to go on the stage. All four Rix children had become interested in the theatre because of their mother, Fanny, who ran an amateur dramatic society and was the lead soprano in the local operatic society. All her children performed in the plays and two of them, Brian and Sheila, became professional actors. Sheila Mercier, as she became known, played Annie Sugden for 25 years in the Yorkshire TV soap opera Emmerdale Farm. Rix performed on stage and TV specialising in a series of post-war "Whitehall farce" comedies, which starred the likes of Tommy Cooper and Sid James. When his eldest daughter, Shelley, was born with Down's syndrome in 1951, he launched a new career, campaigning for people with learning disabilities. He entered the House of Lords as a crossbencher in 1992 and was president of the disability charity Mencap from 1998 until his death in 2016.

Jean Rook was born on 13 November, 1931, the only child of Horace Rook, a consultant engineer, and his wife. The family lived in Hull until 1940, when they moved to North Yorkshire. They moved back to Hull after the war, and she became a pupil at Malet Lambert Grammar School. After school, she decided to go into journalism and subsequently applied for a job on the Hull Daily Mail, but was told she was too old at 25 and that she hadn't "a cat in hell's chance of getting to Fleet Street". However, she got a place on the Sheffield Telegraph's graduate trainee scheme, and her distinctive style of writing won her the job of columnist. She moved to the Yorkshire Post as its Women's Editor, then on to the fashion magazine, "Flair". From "Flair" she was recruited to be fashion editor of the new Sun newspaper. Jean's next move was to the Daily Sketch, which soon merged with the Daily Mail. She was much in demand by this time, and joined the Daily Express. It was there that she was dubbed "The First Lady of Fleet Street", writing a regular column of interviews and opinion.

Lene Lovich, (right) born March 30, 1949, is an American singer, songwriter and musician of Serbian and English descent based in England. She first gained attention in 1979 with the release of her hit single "Lucky Number", which peaked at number 3 on the UK Singles Chart and made her a  leading figure of the new wave music scene. Lovich was born Lili-Marlene Premilovich in Detroit, Michigan, to an English mother and a Serbian father. After her father had health problems, her mother took her and her three siblings to live in Hull. Lovich was 13 years old at the time. She met the guitarist/songwriter Les Chappell when they were teenagers, and he became her longtime collaborator and life partner. In autumn 1968, they went to London to attend art school. It was there that Lovich first tied her hair into the plaits that later became a visual trademark. In her early to mid-20s, she attended several art schools, busked around the London Underground, and amongst other things, appeared in cabaret clubs as an "Oriental" dancer. She also travelled to Spain, where she visited Salvador Dalí in his home.

Clive A. Sullivan MBE (right) born 9 April 1943 in Cardiff, was a Welsh rugby union and professional Rugby League World Cup winning footballer of the 1960s, 70s and 80s. A Great Britain and Wales international winger, he played with both Hull and Hull Kingston Rovers in his career, and also played for Oldham, and Doncaster. He was the first black captain of the Great Britain Lions and for any national British sporting side. Sullivan had an outstanding game and gained the support of the Hull club and city. Sullivan became known for his exceptional speed and the way he would outplay rugby league's finest opposition wingers. His upper-body was deceptively strong which gave him excellent cover defence. Despite his knees which haunted his childhood requiring constant attention and further operations, he played a total of 352 games for Hull, scoring 250 tries. In his 213 games for Hull K.R. he scored 118 tries. Sullivan represented Great Britain 17 times and appeared at three World Cups, 1968 and 1972 with Great Britain and in 1975 for Wales. When Sullivan died of cancer in 1985 aged just 42, the city of Hull held him in such high regard that a section of the city's main approach road (the A63) between the Humber Bridge and the city centre was renamed Clive Sullivan Way in his honour.

Stan Smith was born in 1929 and grew up in a working class family in Hull. Apart from his natural talent for drawing, which he showed early on, few would have predicted the rough, tough baker's son would become Head of Fine Art at Oxford's Ruskin School of Drawing and Fine Art, Honorary Life President of The London Group, Member of the Royal Watercolour Society, Chairman of the Chelsea Arts Club - and a frequent exhibitor at the Royal Academy. Smith wrote and edited several educational books about drawing and painting.

British comedian **Norman Collier** (below) achieved popularity follow-ing television appearances in the 1970s. He was best known for his 'faulty microphone' routine and for his chicken impressions. Collier was born in Hull, into the working-class family of Thomas and Mary (née Dowling) Collier on Christmas Day 1925. He grew up in the centre of Hull as the eldest of eight children. At age 17, he joined the Royal Navy and served as a gunner towards the end of the Second World War. After being demobilised he found work as a labourer. In 1948, while visiting Hull's Perth Street West club, an act failed to turn up, and Collier volunteered to fill in. He felt natural on stage and started to work a few local clubs. While working at BP's chemical factory in Salt End, east of Hull, Collier started making his workmates laugh with improvised comic routines during breaks. Encouraged by his managers, he started to work the wider northern working club scene, becoming a full-time comic in 1962 and enjoying steady success through the 1960s. He was the originator of the 'club chairman' character later popularised by Colin Crompton in the ITV series Wheeltappers and Shunters Club. Collier lived in Welton, a village west of Hull, and was married with three children.

Michael "Mick" Ronson was an English guitarist, songwriter, multi-instrumentalist, arranger, and producer. He achieved critical and commercial success working with David Bowie as one of the Spiders from Mars. He was a session musician who recorded with Bowie followed by several albums with Ian Hunter, also Morrissey, as well as a sideman in touring bands with Van Morrison and Bob Dylan. Michael Ronson was born in Hull in 1946. He joined his first band, The Mariners, in November 1963, when he was 17. His stage debut with The Mariners was in support of the Keith Herd Band at Brough Village Hall, a gig for which the band travelled 35 miles and got paid 10 shillings (50p). While Ronson was working with The Mariners, another local Hull group – The Crestas – recruited him on the advice of The Mariners' bassist John Griffiths. With Ronson on board the Crestas gained a solid reputation, making regular appearances at local halls: Mondays at the Halfway House in Hull, Thursdays at the Ferryboat Hotel, Fridays at the Regal Ballroom in Beverley, and Sundays at the Duke of Cumberland in North Ferriby. Early in 1970, John Cambridge came back to Hull in search of Ronson, intent upon recruiting him for a new David Bowie backing band called The Hype. He found Ronson marking out a rugby pitch, one of his duties as a Parks Department gardener for Hull City Council. Having failed in his earlier attempts in London, Ronson was reluctant, but eventually agreed to accompany Cambridge to a meeting with Bowie. Two days later, on 5 February, Ronson made his debut with Bowie on John Peel's national BBC Radio 1 show.

AT THE SHOPS

The ladies in this photograph look very stylish and elegant in an era when fashion and society were all important. The early 1900s marked the rise of the haute couture movement. Women of the upper classes coveted the Parisian designs, which set the tone for the rest of the Western fashion world. Powolny's on King Edward Street was in the middle of an ornately-designed parade of shops and catered specifically for this type of customer. Renowned for its luxurious and glamorous setting and a cuisine masterminded by continental chefs, Polly's, as it was affectionately known, was one of the city's major cultural and social attractions. Complete with marble flooring, mahogany doors and oak paneling, it opened in 1903.

Next door is the Lipton's Tea Shop which was owned by Thomas Johnstone Lipton. From humble beginnings in Glasgow in the 1870s, the stores had begun to appear throughout Britain and "Lipton's" became a household name. To the left, we can see the newly opened retail sports outlet of the Asbestos And Rubber Company Ltd. Some three decades later, the firm expanded into the supply and fixing of rubber floor coverings, asbestos heat insulating materials and fibre acoustic insulation (see the story on p146). Sadly, these building were the victim of a German bombing raid in May 1941.

Right: The corner shop has been a British institution for hundreds of years. In the early nineteenth century when French leader Napoleon was asked what he thought of the UK he famously replied: "Britain is nothing more than a nation of shopkeepers."

At the time Napoleon made his comment there was only one kind of shop in Britain, small shops independently run by a family who lived above the premises. Perhaps only our older readers will recognise these two photographs from the old Jacksons store at Spring Bank (exterior) and Inglemire Lane (interior). It was 1851 when William Jackson first set up as a grocer in Scale Lane, in Hull's old town, later moving to Carr Lane. Eventually his shops occupied prime corner sites throughout Yorkshire and the North Midlands. The first bakery opened in 1891 and the current Jackson's bakery on Derringham Street opened in 1907. There was no self service, when this internal shot was taken, a customers chair was a fixture in most shops. The stores were immactulately clean tidy and well organised and everything had its place.

Below: The two children seen here in this photograph are George Empson and his sister Hilda, outside their father's fried fish and potatoes shop in Argyle Street, Hull. Fish and chip shops were originally small family businesses, often run from the 'front room' of the house and were commonplace by the late 19th century. Through the latter part of the 19th century and well into the 20th century, the fish and chip trade expanded greatly to satisfy the needs of the growing industrial population of Great Britain. The development of the steam trawler brought fish from all over the North Atlantic, Iceland and Greenland and the steam railways allowed easy and fast distribution of the fish around the country. This might have been one of the earliest shops of this type in Hull and we can see that the business was branching out in several other areas of the city as well. Haddock and Plaice were on the menu for customers but salt and ice was also available at the family run business.

Known as "The Harrods of the North", Carmichael's was Hull's premier upmarket department store for much of the 20th Century and about the closest you could get to a real-life Are You Being Served? Sadly, the George Street store closed for the final time in 1991 after 89 years of trading. For Hull shoppers, one store stood above the rest when it came to finding the most elegant china, the most exclusive jewellery and the latest fashions from Paris and London. The Carmichael story began in 1902 when Robert Carmichael and his brothers Herbert, James and Arthur, went into business together.

Owned by the family of Hull-born actor Ian Carmichael until 1962, the firm was taken over by Woolworths before being bought out in February 1989 by its then manager Rosemary Edwards and accountant Pal Gill. Their aim was to make Carmichaels more than just the best luxury store in the north, but to rival the great fashion and furnishing houses of London. But their dream was to remain just that. Changing times and a government squeeze on consumer spending were to combine to spell an end to one of Hull's most famous stores in January 1991.

This is a sight not seen in modern photographs of Paragon Square. The aesthetically pleasing pre-war building in the picture is Hammond's department store, an institution that has been an integral part of Hull's history, since the early 19th century. In 1821, H.W. Hammond opened a drapery shop on the old North Bridge. The business continued to operate at this location until 1861, when the store moved to Osborne Street. In 1889 the business was sold to James Powell and his three sons, whose family continued to operate the business until 1972. By 1916, a splendid new building was opened in Paragon Square. We can see the exterior of the new building in this photograph from 1937; a place where customers could meet their friends and enjoy a meal. A trip to the department store had become a day out. Disaster struck however, in 1941, when the elegant store was largely destroyed by German bombing. Hull mourned the loss of the Hammonds store, but within a week, 47 of the store's departments were open again in a temporary location.

The store that was classed as an institution in Hull was rebuilt in 1952 on Paragon Square, with extensions added in 1954 and 1957. Within a couple of years the business had grown again by opening its own hairdressing salon, and in 1960 added a new warehouse to accommodate their furniture workshops and stock rooms. In the second photograph we can see the Christmas decorations outside the store in December of the same year.

This nostalgic photograph from the early 1960s shows a fabulous array of shops along King Edward Street on a bright summers day. Much of the area in view, has been pedestrianised in recent years, with big trees lining the streets. In the 50s and 60s the average man bought a new suit every couple of years, and in 1965 the menswear industry sold thirteen million suits. The most well known and most prolific was Montague Burton, but other high street chains included the Fifty Shilling Tailor, John Temple, Dunn & Co and Alexandre, who had the prime corner site at the time of this photograph. The shop later became a branch of Dolland & Aitchison opticians. The No63 trolleybus looks to be pulling out behind the three ladies on pushbikes waiting at the junction. We can just make out the policeman on duty, on the corner of the traffic island. To the right, the cars heading into Savile Street include a three-wheel BMW Isetta followed by an Austin A40.

Here we can see two pictures of Tivoli House taken in different decades. On the corner of South Street and Paragon Street, the property is "typical of its era" with a concrete frame and curtained walls. The 1960s office block, was built on the site of the Tivoli Theatre which was demolished in 1959. In the earliest photograph, is a large rectangular panel clad in coloured bricks, with the name Tivoli House in big letters. Underneath, is one of the original tenants of the ground floor retail unit, the Wimpy Bar. Long before McDonald's, the much-missed restaurant was the first to bring US-style hamburger meals to Hull in the 1950s and 60s. In the second image, a Hull institution had taken over the unit. Skeltons Bakery, was founded in 1931 and grew to have 43 shops and eight cafés across East Yorkshire and Lincolnshire.

Known for its savouries and cakes, including apple doughnuts and Maids of Honour. Prior to being vacated around twelve years ago, the upper floors of the building were occupied by the local government.

Below: There is nothing familiar today, to compare to this photgraph from the junction of King Edward Street and Jameson Street in the 1930s. The only building still recognisable is the Victorian Grade II* listed Dock Offices, on the right, which is now home to the Maritime Museum. The part of King Edward Street directly ahead is now pedestrianised and treelined and miles away from the scene we see here, with the wide thoroughfare filled with cars, trams and bicycles. Despite the policeman in the white coat on traffic duty, people seem to be wandering across the busy junction without any heed to the traffic. Dolcis Shoes shops had begun to appear on the high street in the UK after the company went public in 1930. It is believed that the name is taken from a Swiss sock stamp.

Below: This view of Fletchers Corner, before pedestrianisation, was probably captured in the early 1960s. A policeman directs traffic flow from his central island box, across from Fletchers well known delicatessen. Fletchers' flagship store opened in November 1956; the large building that swept around the corner of Jameson Street and King Edward Street. Before Greggs and Cooplands, regional bakery chains like, Fletchers, Skeltons and McLeish were having a right bun fight to gain supremacy in the city. This was great for all of us who liked our cakes, buns and pasties.

On the corner, directly in front of Fletchers, was the Penny Fountain, which delighted generations of children and visitors. In its first two years in the 1950s, throwing coins for wishes, £2,000 worth of coins were collected, which were used to pay for an outing for senior citizens.

It is hard to believe, but it is over 60 years ago since this photograph was taken looking along Brook Street. Taken from an elevated position in the Yorkshire Electricity building on Ferensway, much has changed in terms of the road layout, but the main buildings have remained much the same. Traditional car manufacturers seem to dominate the roads at that time with little of the continental influence. Dominant in the picture are Ford, Austin and Morris makes of car. The big display window on the corner is Trippets, an old established family drapery business, that later years, became Argos and more recently was part of a coffee shop chain. Further along Brook Street, is Prout's and then Bloom's gentlemens outfitters. On the right would have been the Broadway Hotel and the Shire Horse.

We can tell from the open windows on the British Home Stores (BHS) building, it was a hot day for a change, when this photograph was taken well over 50 years ago in Hull. Looking on from Silver Street along Whitefriargate the very distinctive Bhs building style is still recognisable today, although it is now the premises of Superdrug. British Home Stores run by a group of US entrepreneurs opened a store in Brixton in 1928 selling lighting and food with the aim of emulating Woolworths. Initially, nothing cost more than a shilling. Almost 90 years later, a tide of nostalgia for the British brand was unleashed when BHS collapsed in 2016, The BHS store (once a Co-Op) now in Jameson Street was among the chain's 163 British shops that were earmarked for closure. Retail experts say the BHS collapse is the biggest high street failure since Woolworths' demise in 2008.

In the Middle Ages there were friars in Hull. Friars were like monks but instead of withdrawing from the world they went out to preach. Carmelite Friars (known as white friars because of the colour of their habits) arrived in 1293. They live on, of course, in the street name Whitefriargate.

WHEN WE WERE YOUNG

This is a charming and picturesque photograph from the early part of the 20th century, taken on the side of the lake in West Park. A popular pastime was to come down and feed the ducks and swans and this group of four young children has certainly grabbed the attention of at least one of the swans who resides on the lake. The land on which West Park is now situated was acquired by the Corporation from the North Eastern Railway Company in 1878. It was not until 1885 that the 'Western Disctrict Park', as it had been initially called, was officially opened by the Mayor, A. K. Rollit.

The park, on a large site on Anlaby Road and Walton Street, encompasses 31 acres and was designed by Mr Joseph Fox Sharpe, Borough Engineer, with the project providing work for 200 unemployed men. The rustic footbridge over the lake can be seen in the background which led to an island feature and bandstand. The lake was converted into a childrens play area and paddling pool around 60 years agp and is now the site of an adverture playground and miniture railway track.

Right: On a day when people can sit out and enjoy the milder weather, onlookers watch as a man leans precariously over the stone barrier, as it appears he is trying to retrieve something from the lake in Pearson Park. The park was originally known as 'The People's Park' in the west of Hull. It is situated about 1 mile (1.5 km) north-west of the city centre of Hull with its main entrance on Beverley Road and its western boundary adjoining Princes Avenue. The original park design was by J. C. Niven and established through the gift of land by Zachariah

Pearson. It was the first public park in the city and originally included a cricket ground, a folly.... 'The Ruins', a statue of Ceres, the goddess, as well as the lake. Other early features surviving included a cast iron drinking fountain and statues of Queen Victoria and Prince Albert, both by Thomas Earle. A bandstand was installed in 1908.

Below: It has to be said that these youngsters look a little too well dressed for a snowball fight, even back in 1904. It is though, a very pretty scene of the entrance to Pearson Park in Hull, and still very recognisable today. This group of young girls have almost built a small snowman and may have just returned from Sunday school or a local church service. Erected in the 1860s the archway and gates we see here provided a grand entrance to the park, sadly the gates are likely to have been 'confiscated' for the war effort in the 1940s, so this grand entrance lacks a little from its former glory. Development of the high quality 'villa' residences on the road took place throughout the latter part of the 19th century, as we can see in this photograph.

Right: Quite a crowd had gathered to see these children cascading down the new water shute at East Park, Hull, in 1929, after all it would have been one of the first in the country. The park was opened in 1887 on Queen Victoria's Jubilee and, the Ferens Boating Lake proved a great attraction with the public. Local councillors felt more use could be made of the lake and tenders went out in 1928 for the installation of a new 'water shute' or 'splash boat' as it later became known. Once approved, the tower and runway into the lake were constructed, with a height drop of 22 feet and a runway

from start to finish of about 100 feet, it was an immediate hit with local children. The shute continues today thanks to an extensive restoration in 2011 and the English Heritage Grade II listing. Lets hope local children continue to enjoy the 'splash boat' for many years to come.

Below: These young lads look very well behaved at the side of the lake at Pearsons Park around 1911. One young chap is holding what appears to be a dolls pram, ensuring the doll inside is shaded from the sun with a pram cover, the other lads are 'fishing for tiddlers' at the side. Again they are all well dressed in their Sunday best and are no doubt keen to keep it that way and avoid their parents wrath.

Above: Another lovely scene of three young girls standing alongside the lake at East Park in Hull, with four swans interested to see if they might pick up a few morsels of bread. The girls are certainly focused on the swans and there seems to be a bit of a stand off situation at the time the photograph was taken. The girls dressed in their finery of smock type dresses and hats; seem unaware of the onlookers on the bridge in the distance. They look like they are standing at the edge of Ferens boating lake, which is one of the surviving features from the era. It was established on land donated by T.R. Ferens in 1913 and extended in 1923, a double arched bridge with decorative balustrades built around 1925.

Right: An appropriate title for this old photograph could be 'Cakes and Angels', as this angelic group of youngsters from Hull, pose in front of a table full of homemade sweet delights. The group in the centre, of mainly girls, look very smart in their Sunday best white party frocks. We can see from the children on the outside of the group, that it was fashionable in the early 1900s, for upper and middle class boys to wear stiff, detachable collars which folded flat over the tops of their jackets or waistcoats. They were called 'Eton collars' because they imitated the uniform of the boys at the wealthy Eton College. Working class boys usually wore collarless shirts with a V-neck woollen pullover. Whatever the occasion, it is certainly a special one!

Above and below: Davy Crockett in Hull on horseback in the middle of the day? Not an expected scene for those leaving the National Provincial Bank or wandering along the street, considering which shop to visit next. The reasons for this bizarre scene were very much down to Humberside Police who in 1955 decided to follow the popular theme from the recent Hollywood film of Davy Crockett to get their message across to youngsters about road safety. There were 27,000 road related injuries nationally each month in 1954 and the police were looking for innovative ways to reduce these numbers dramatically. The great frontiersman was seen as the ideal character to reach children and adults alike across Kingston upon Hull in the days when film stars and the stories the portrayed were always believed in. The message was spread across the schools and playgrounds of Hull with 'Davy Crockett' visiting them to pass on the ways how not to become one of those many casualties and no doubt delivered in a strong, drawling American mid west accent. Although the next photograph doesn't quite support that road safety theme, with 'Davy Crockett' sat on the kerb of a busy duel carriageway, chatting to a young lad with his dog, the horse seems to be enjoying the grass verge!

Children always loved and ice cream and still do, regardless of whether it was made by a champion producer or not. Padgett and Sons had recently won first prize in a national ice cream competition in October 1956 in Wales and they had a healthy number of customers, even though it was grey and wet day at the Hull Fair. You could either go inside for the cafeteria and maybe sit with

a warm coffee, or be served outside at very reasonable prices or they even had a self-service section which no doubt the lad on the left had had a go at trying to load his threepenny cone with as much ice cream as he could. It was no doubt that the children of Hull would sample the award winning local ice cream as often as their mum's would allow.

Above and below: Cod liver oil, it was the bain of most children's lives at the end of the war. Given that a group of trawler owners from Hull, started they British Cod Liver Oil Producers Company in Hull in 1934, the children had no escape! It had been known to have medicinal benefits for many years before being tested scientifically in the 1920s and confirmed as having extremely beneficial properties. The Norwegians had previously supplied the vast majority of Cod Liver Oil, with 40000 fish being needed to produce 4000 gallons of oil, but the new company with its refinery in Marfleet, Hull would go on to supply the UK market.

During the second world war, Cod Liver Oil was produced for the Ministry of Food under a free distribution scheme to all children up to the age of five and pregnant women and nursing mothers. With this growth in the market, the Seven Seas brand became synonymous with health products and capsules.

We can see the expansion of the company in the exhibition photograph from the Blackpool Exhibition in 1953.

The children in this photo are putting on a good show as taking a spoonful of cod liver oil was only memorable for its awful taste, texture and lingering aftertaste.

Water has always held a fascination for the young, but this scene would sadly be frowned upon today. The photograph was taken in the 1930s in the 'timber pools' next to the Victoria Dock in Hull. The lads had taken to the rafts like 'ducks to water' and were happy enough, punting their way around the pools playing 'Swallows and Amazons' or pirates of the Caribbean. They will have reached their craft by precariously making their way across the floating timber, possibly discarded by the timber merchants at the docks as the trade had grown dramatically in the preceding years. The lads dressed in jackets, short trousers and woolly socks appear to be pretty good at keeping dry, so the rafts must be stable and their balance will have been honed as this was no doubt a regular occurance. A fabulous photograph of lads at play, while the girls stay at home playing with their dolls.

Right: At the time of this photograph, it would have been a wonderful and a long anticipated relief for these young children to finally take part in a parade at the end of WWII. Not just in Hull, but children up and down the country, had endured years of austerity, rationing and fear through the recent war years. They are smiling here though, in the parade through the centre of Hull, celebrating the declaration of victory in 1945. Parents had gone to great lengths to dress

them in costumes, old frocks, kilts and hats to make it the best occasion possible, both for those taking part and the many onlookers who crowded the streets. Similar celebrations had erupted across the country as Germany finally surrendered on 7 May, 1945 and a public holiday was declared for VE Day.

Below: Company Christmas parties for their employees children, were a very popular way for employers to say thank you to staff for all their hard work over the previous 12 months, and they proved extremely popular with the children too! Some companies would arrange a trip to the local pantomime with gifts and sweets for the journey while others would send parcels home to be opened on Christmas Day. Clearly these children, whose parents worked at Electro-Furnace Products in 1960, were very much enjoying their party, which would no doubt have included cakes, jelly and ice cream and plenty of fizzy drinks. Entertainment would probably include a clown or magician and of course the much awaited visit from Santa. These young ones are raring to have a go at pulling crackers and look every bit the part in their Sunday best and party hats.

Peter Hird & Sons
Specialists within the access platform and lifting industry

Back in January, 1983, Peter Hird & Sons Ltd started trading in Hull having been formed by husband and wife team Peter and Christine Hird.

Fast forward to 2017 and what was once a little known company is now a nationally known brand and employer with links across the world.

Peter Hird would become a well-known figure in the cranes and access industries, having rented both cranes and access platforms for many years. He would become probably best known, however, for his attention to the technical detail of the products that his company bought for its rental fleet.

In the mid-1980s he developed a comparative test for electric battery powered work platforms. This became known worldwide as the "Hird test" and is still used in many facilities today. He was also responsible for a number of small but very practical ideas that platform producers adopted into their machines

Peter was born in 1939, in Malton, North Yorkshire. In the late 1950s he was called up for National Service and joined the army, serving in the Royal Engineers

After leaving the army in December, 1959, Peter worked on large construction sites abroad for several years in Europe. He returned to the UK and more specifically Hull to work as a bulldozer driver in 1964.

Working for a period of time as a bulldozer driver, and later a sales representative, Peter eventually gave into his own aspirations of one day owning and running his own company.

In 1975, he went into business with the Horncastle Group and set up Fleet Lifting Services which was run from a depot located on Itlings Lane in Hessle, supplying the local area with access platforms and small items of plant. However it

Above: Peter Hird vehicles lifting a bridge into place on Hedon Road. Below: Company founder Peter Hird.

was not long until Peter started to get itchy feet and wanted to break free of the partnership and do business his own way.

So, on November 17, 1982, the company name of Peter Hird & Sons Ltd was formed and it was time for Peter to push on with dreams of been his own boss.

Then, on January 23, 1983, Peter Hird & Sons officially started trading, with the help of his wife, Christine, and backing from the local bank, Peter now had control over his own destiny. With his initial loan Peter bought second hand equipment: an iron fairy crane, a fork lift truck, a crane lorry, three vehicle-mounted access platforms and a van, and began offering machinery removals.

He gradually added more cranes from the likes of Hydracon, Cosmos and Coles. In the early stages the company was predominantly a mobile crane hire company with a sizeable fleet topped by a 30 tonne Coles; but as demand grew for platforms in the late 1980s the company acquired a few Simon Snorkel truck-mounted lifts and a Pegasus dumper-based platform

Above: A Coles Mobile crane. Right: Managing director Philip Hird. Bottom: Part of the early lifting fleet.

which proved popular with local tree surgeons as well as painters and decorators.

In 1991 the company won the Training Enterprise Council's business award for Quality of Service through Training – beating competition from several major industrial names in Hull to gain the accolade. The active promotion of safe working practices has from the outset been a key part of the company's progress. The HSE-supported Humberside Health and Safety Group elected Peter as its President for a three year term.

In 1997 Mr Hird's son, Philip Hird, now the current managing director, joined the company at age 15 working as a mechanical fitter. With his father and the rest of the team behind him Philip furthered his career and worked his way through various departments of the business. He even spent time as a crane operator during the building of the St Stephens Shopping centre that is now one of Hull's biggest retail outlets.

Finally, at the age of 65, Peter Hird retired from the company, after putting in the foundations to form what is now a nationally recognised brand. When he retired, the company had grown considerably and, from been a very small firm with minimal equipment and a lot of passion, it had reached proportions well above what Peter Hird had ever expected in the early days.

In 2008 the company saw an opportunity to expand into a new area and their Doncaster, or now aptly named Central Hub, opened, more access platforms where acquired and Peter Hird & Sons went to work on growing the new branch, but the happiness was short lived.

In 2009 the company fell on hard times due to mismanagement forcing the company to sell the remaining fleet of its mobile cranes in order to keep the business going.

"Watching the cranes leave the yard for one last time was difficult" said Philip, who at the time was working as the company's site representative. "Cranes where in my blood and I had grown up around them from being two-years-old."

However, the sale of the cranes only made the team more determined and passionate to return the company to its former state.

Philip later secured a major contract with a client, to supply all the mini cranes to a new project located in London. The cranes were used to install curtain walling panels (glazing) onto a 72-storey skyscraper, which became known as The Shard; now Europe's tallest building. Its construction began in March 2009; it was topped out on 30 March, 2012, and formally opened on 5 July, 2012. It opened to the public on 1 February, 2013. Standing 309.6 metres (1,016 ft.) high, the Shard is the tallest building in the European Union. It is also the second-tallest free-standing structure in the United Kingdom, second only to the concrete tower of the Emley Moor television transmitting station.

Philip worked tirelessly on the project devoting much of his time to supplying the building project with the equipment needed but things were about to change. The supply of the equipment to the Shard building project also brought in many new customers from the South of England; it was time for the Hird brand to expand so in 2010 the company opened up a new facility in Redhill, Surrey, just south of London. The southern depot focuses on supplying the building boom in London and surrounding areas and offered the company a more cost effective approach and better response to its customers'

Right: A Grove Scissor is able to reach heights of 38ft.

Above: Peter Hird & Sons have installed glazing on The Shard in London. Below: Workers use a Valla crane and vacuum lifter to safely install glass.

needs. In 2011, Philip Hird was appointed as Managing Director and a new fresh outlook was born.

In January 2011 a storm hit Hull with wind gusts up to 100mph, many people and buildings were affected by the gusts and large amounts of damage was recorded. Peter Hird & Sons didn't get away lightly either. The company has operated its maintenance workshops out of three interconnecting buildings since 1983. The buildings dated back to the 1800's and had once housed a blacksmiths and horses for pulling the boats and goods up and down the docks. On that fateful day in 2011 the winds destroyed the building roof and made the buildings unsafe to occupy. The company had to setup a temporary workshop inside a marque in the yard area whilst the unsafe roof was removed until designers could come up with a plan for the replacement. Nearly two years later and the roof had been removed, redesigned and re-fitted, the work-shops had been modernised and were nearly ready to be operational again.

Another problem was just around the corner, though - the floods of December 2013 hit, the company based on English Street was flooded by the tidal surge that affected much of the city on that December night. The newly refurbished workshops were damaged, many of the company's machines where flooded and not repairable, and approximately three feet of water had entered into the company's training

Left: Hull Marina speedboat racing in the early 90's. *Above:* Hird crane lifting machinery in the late 80's.

centre making it un-useable. Worst still the company's offices where destroyed. All the office equipment was flooded.

"We lost all our computers," said Philip. "Our telephone system was gone, our paperwork was just a sodden pile and everything we needed to operate was destroyed. The day after the floods receded the staff got to work, telephone calls where re-directed to the company's other depots, emails where sent to mobile phones and the old fashioned pen and paper way of running a business came back to life."

Below: Some of the modern range of equipment used by Peter Hird & Sons.

Over the forthcoming weeks the company installed temporary offices onto the site, washed away the silt and mud from the flooding and started to pick themselves back up. Repairs where done where possible and lots of effort went into putting the site back onto its feet. Unfortunately the main offices were flooded and damaged beyond repair eventually leading to them been torn down and replaced with a car park facility.

Over the next couple of years Philip and the directors worked on building up the company and placing it onto better footings within the construction industry. As time passed the company expanded into new product lines; more staff were employed and the Hird brand became a nationally recognised company.

In early 2014, the struggles of recent years were placed firmly in the past when Philip had a surreal experience. He was working

in the Surrey area and as he drove down the road he noticed a familiar sight. As he drove closer towards a construction site, there working with its full jib extended was one of the mobile cranes the company had to sell in 2009.

"The crane still had the company name written on the jib for everyone to see," he said. After stopping and visiting the site where the crane was, he received a phone call from the gentleman who had purchased the crane in 2009. The crane was for sale and Philip was the first person given the opportunity to buy it. Four months later the crane was delivered back to its home in Hull.

"We couldn't believe we had done it, we'd turned the company around, survived major damage to buildings and a catastrophic flood then had purchased back what was once the flagship of the company," said Philip.

Far more was still to come from the company though. It expanded massively in all its product lines, each week new equipment was added to the vast amount which had been built up since 2009.

Above: *Teaching operators how to use the equipment at Peter Hird & Sons in the early 90's.*

Then, in 2015, the biggest single purchase the company had ever made happened – it bought a brand new 100 tonne mobile crane

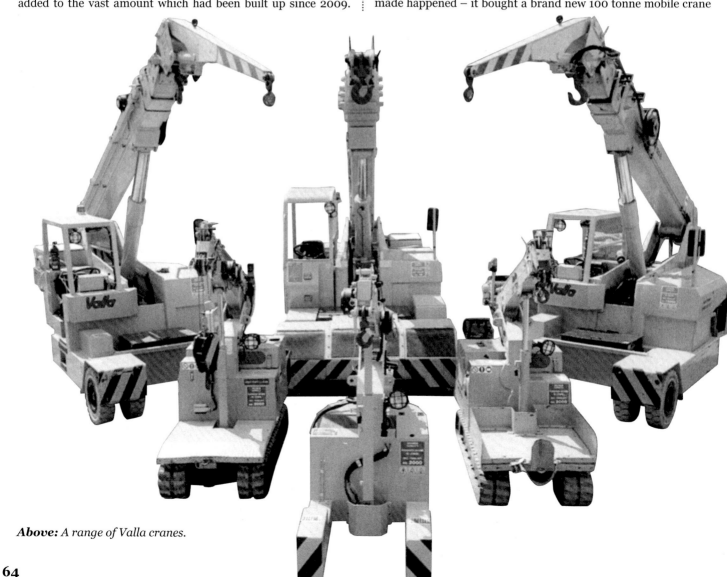

Above: *A range of Valla cranes.*

Above: *Gerry Welford (left), Manitowoc UK sales manager is pictured handing over the Grove GMK4100L to Phil Hird (right).*

from a manufacturer in Germany. The new Grove 4100L crane is huge, weighing more than 30 average family cars and has now become the new flagship and proudly displays the company name.

So, after all the ups and downs, the company has faced over its many years of history, the later years have been its most exciting. From humble beginnings in 1983, it has now more than 30 years' experience, employs more 90 people and is continuing to expand on a daily basis.

Peter Hird & sons now has three main locations in the UK but works with suppliers and customers from across the world and now supplies

some of the best known brands like Virgin Atlantic, BAE Systems, Airbus, and many more. Products are even sold as far away as Brazil and Kuwait.

But, Hull will always be its home and to further cement its place in the city the company was proud to be voted the 'Medium Business of the Year 2016', at the Hull Daily Mail awards.

Right: *Peter Hird & Sons collecting the award for Medium Business of the Year 2016.*

THE WAR YEARS AND BEYOND

Hull suffered particularly badly in the early years of the Second World War, which killed hundreds of people and left hundreds of thousands of pounds worth of damage. A major raid occurred on the night 18 March, 1941, one of several large raids that spring, although it had been frequently bombed since the summer of 1940 and would continue to be a target into 1943. For security reasons, journalists were only allowed to refer to bombing in a 'north east costal town' so the rest of the country remained unaware of the fact that ninety five percent of houses were damaged and Hull was the most severely damaged city or town in the UK. Almost half the population being made homeless, around 152,000 were affected. Around 38,000 children were evacuated from Hull to East Yorkshire, Lincolnshire, Lancashire, Norfolk and North-

umberland. This photograph shows a group of rescue workers who have helped to clear a bombsite on Ferensway. The mangled motorbike and lorry are testament to the devastation which took place. The next photo shows a similar scene of carnage on Prospect Street, when bombing damaged the Hull Infirmary in 1941. The old Hull Royal Infirmary, Prospect Street, opened in September 1784, and was roughly where the Prospect Centre now stands, between Prospect Street, Brook Street and Mill Street.

The concept of the Kite Barge was straight forward enough, they would be sailed or towed into position with the barrage balloon raised as high as possible to deter enemy aircraft attacks on shipping and the harbour infrastructure. Enemy aircraft were also seeking to drop sea-mines and had to fly low to achieve the accuracy needed. The principle had worked well on land and the war military had decided that waterborne balloons should work equally as well. Harbours and estuaries were prime targets for the enemy, both to destroy vessels and to disrupt the flow on military and supply ships. Trawlers and Drifters were often commandeered to provide the flat base and winch system required to bed the balloon during sailing. The barge seen here was an ideal structure for the balloons although the sailors and RAF men who were needed to man the vessels may have disagreed, due to the confined sleeping and eating arrangements. Here we see a typical Kite Barge in ther Hull estuary around 1943. A land photograph shows the use of a barrage balloon in the centre of Hull around the same time, with a fairly unsurprised cyclist passing beneath it, no doubt having seen it all before.

In the late 1930s urgent plans were made for the defence of our citizens on the home front. The lessons of the civil war in Spain when historic towns like Guernica were removed from the map by aerial bombardment brought home to everyone that the next major conflict would not be confined to traditional battlefields. Fortunately, not everyone believed in Mr Chamberlain's little piece of paper that he brought back from Berlin in 1938, proclaiming 'peace in our time'. The lessons of the brutal invasion of Czechoslovakia shortly afterwards were well learned. Civil defence groups were founded and put on a war footing. The Air Raid Precautions (ARP) people were galvanised into action, organising dummy runs to teach us self preservation in case of an air raid and, more worryingly, how to survive an attack from chemical weapons. For those of us who listened to the US president in 2003, warning about the potential for such hardware in Iraq, we could say that we had heard it all before. In World War I many thousands of soldiers were gassed in the trenches and, as World War II loomed, it was feared that aeroplanes might drop gas bombs, containing mustard, phosgene, chlorine and a host of other horrors that we had never even heard about, on our cities. During the summer of 1939, masks were issued to the most vulnerable and advice on their use given at classes run by the ARP.

It was on the 8 May, 1945, that the Prime Minister, Winston Churchill, sat in the Cabinet room at No.10 Downing Street and announced, through a radio broadcast to the whole of Britain, that a ceasefire had been signed the previous day. This was Victory in Europe (VE) day and those soldiers, nurses and families who had endured some 2,074 days of war, cheered and celebrated the end of this terrible conflict. Churchill had said this victory was the peoples victory and "... neither the long years, nor the dangers, nor the fierce attacks of the enemy, have in any way weakened the independent resolve of the British nation...". There was a steely determination and sacrifice by those at home. People were indeed proud to have come through the war, but many had lost loved ones, friends, homes and possessions and knew it would be some years before Britain was able to get back on its feet. Lives had changed for both men, women and especially children, many who had been evacuated to homes many miles away for their own safety.

Despite all this hardship and misery, this was a time of jubilation and relief. In these photos we can see members of a Hull family at home, listening to the Prime Ministers message on the radio. Mum and young baby could for once smile again and perhaps now look forward to a more stable and prosperous future. The soldiers and nurses pictured left in the hospital seem more pensive about the good news. Maybe it is a time for reflection, considering their future and those they have left behind or lost during the war.

Later, services, memorials and parades would take place to commemorate colleagues and provide a fitting tribute to them. But for this day in May 1945, people could celebrate and so they did.

One such parade of scouts, guides, brownies and children in fancy dress, took place in Hull some weeks later. It was a proud and thankful gathering by the children of Hull who wanted to pay their respects and also say thank you to all those who had fought to ensure their future was free from tyranny and oppression.

Riverside Quay was the stopping place for this LNER train and was a welcome sight for the final leg of a long journey, as these tired troops return from war duty. Kitbags held all their possessions from the months or years as they had served their country. A few officers can been seen helping to co-ordinate the embarkation of these troops, who would be both thrilled and anxious about seeing their loved ones and relatives, who would themselves have changed over their enforced absence. It would have taken sometime for them to be fully reconciled and comfortable in each others presence. War can be and has been proven to be a deeply scarring experience for many soldiers. Of course, nothing can prepare them for warfare, seeing close friends die and narrowly escape death themselves. Food shortages, displacement from homes and the loss of relatives all created a toxic legacy that was still being felt for decades after fighting ceased in May 1945.

By the 1950s, the young lads scrambling around the wheels and undercarriage of this Spitfire, had only heard about the exploits of the 'Battle of Britain' pilots from their parents. They were born in the years after those brave young men took to the skies in their epic duels with all the might that Goering's Luftwaffe had to offer. The RAF defended the United Kingdom against the German Air Force attacks from the end of June 1940. At the sound of the cry to scramble he had rushed across the tarmac, signalled for 'chocks away' and powered his Supermarine marvel of modern engineering up to a dogfight that was both exhilarating and frightening. In those wartime years we relied heavily on the few that Churchill saluted in his famous speech about human conflict. Men not long out of boyhood grew up in a few short months as they defended our shores. This exhibition had been appropriately set up on an old bombsite and, whilst being a reminder of the war and the sacrifices that had been made, it was also a recruitment drive for the RAF. The van to the rear had officers sitting at desks waiting to sign up new flying aces like Johnnie Johnson and Douglas Bader. From the mid-1950s, the majority of those who signed up for Regular service were unemployed or not in apprenticeships, so looked on military service as a 'Job' The Royal Air Force station was situated in the suburb of Sutton-on-Hull that operated from 1938 to 1961.

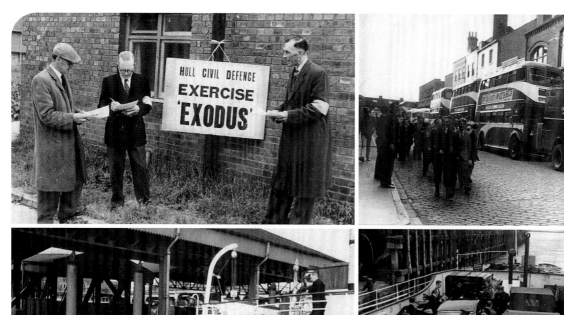

I   t was designed as a practice to evacuate the city of Kingston upon Hull in the event of a catastrophic incident. Exercise 'Exodus' in May 1961 was instigated by the Hull Civil Defence Authority and took place at the height of the Cold War, shortly after the 'Bay of Pigs' incidents in Cuba, where Russia had set-up missile launch sites with the US in range. The exercise involved volunteers, as well as civil defence and emergency personnel, with the public volunteers being evacuated by a fleet of buses and then across the River Humber on ferries.

These chaps are studying their control sheets and evacuation plans, whilst other, with loud halers in hand would ensure their instructions could be heard.

Central co-ordination form the control room was crucial and would ensure that plans at each stage and critical point were in line and on time.

The army were also involved and Jeeps with motorbike outriders gathered in one street to discuss their own co-ordination of transport through this unique event.

Food and a hot drink had been prepared for the hungry volunteers at the dockside, before they were required to board the ferries, although its unlikely in any real event that this would take place.

Boarding the ferries appears orderly and well co-ordinated, but then there was no panic or fear that the ferry would be full before you and your family could board. The service men and women now on board could relax and light a cigarette, whilst officers chatted about the days events and the success and learning they could gather from such a unique exercise.

ENTERTAINMENTS, LEISURE & PASTIMES

Left: The signs says, 'Chicken Joe the man you all know', which is not strictly true. Until the 1960s Chicken Joe was a legend in the North of England, but ask the folk of Hull who Chicken Joe really was and they wouldn't have a clue; he was just Chicken Joe!

His real name was Joe Barak, born in the East End of London in 1898. Joe became a true showman based in Yorkshire, who regularly attended Hull Fair in the 1930s and 1940s, and ran a spinner stall for Ling's Family amusements. One of the main differences between this stall and others is that the prizes on offer were groceries and a fresh chicken. With the gift of the gab he knew exactly how to draw the crowds; sometimes it was almost impossible to get near to his stall. Some readers may also remember the excitement of his weekly draw held at the end of a big fair when all the prizewinners' names went into a hat to win a piano, three piece suite or a sideboard.

Right and below: In 1888, Hull Fair moved to its present home on Walton Street, with the original eight acre site doubling in size in 1906, making it the largest fair in England. By the end of the 19th century, the new fairground site flourished and the popular circus and illusion shows competed with the increasingly fashionable steam powered roundabouts. Punters visiting the fair during this period would have perhaps enjoyed a ride on Green's Switchback Gallopers, Marshall's Bicycles or Tuby's Galloping Horses. Those

who preferred the then traditional attractions offered by the exhibition shows would have attended Proctors and Baileys Circus or William's Ghost Show. The Manders family brought "Hollywood to Hull", with their travelling circus. A popular exhibit of the latter was a tableau of the 'Last Supper' which was contained in its own box-van. In 1899, moving pictures were added to the waxworks exhibition. The show was then renamed "Manders Royal Waxworks & Edison's Electric Animated Pictures".

The glitz and glamour of the circus has seduced audiences across Britain for more than 200 years, bringing an irresistible combination of beauty, skill and danger. The family-run Fossett's Circus has survived two world wars, silent movies, five generations and the invention of the Xbox and Netflix. The 125-year-old circus is believed to be the oldest in the world. The circus's earliest mention was in April, 1888, in an edition of the 'Wicklow People' newspaper. The thrill of watching lions, tigers and elephants prowling the ring, made audiences flock to circuses across Britain

Around the time of this photograph, Negus the tightrope walking lion was a star attraction at Bertram Mills' Circus at Olympia. The circus also saw a resurgence in popularity after the Second World War as people sought an escape from the austerity of everyday life. Hundreds of Hull folk, both adults and children, would have been happy to pay 1/- 6p to be entertained by a wide variety of professional performers, including clowns, acrobats and jugglers.

East Park was first opened to the public on 21 June, 1887, the day the country celebrated Queen Victoria's Golden Jubilee. About 20 years earlier, in the west of the city, Zachariah Pearson had established Hull's first public park. Now comprising approximately 120 acres on the north side of Holderness Road, East Park is the largest of Hull's parks and is often used for large open-air venues such as concerts and the annual Hull Show. In 1900 a 'children's mound' was created in the central section of the park which included rockwork and tunnels. Thomas Ferens presented the land for the boating lake, to the north of the park, to the city in 1913 so linking the park with the adjacent King George V playing fields. The boating lake was extended in 1923 and by 1926 a model yacht pond had been made in the north-west corner of the park. Additional land to the north of the lake and at the eastern end of the park was acquired as the result of the development of the north-east ring road in the 1920s. The park is today an English Heritage Grade 2 listed site. This includes a rare water chute dating from 1929.

Right: Pickering Park on the north side of Hessle Road, was presented to the corporation by Christopher Pickering, opening on 13 July, 1911, part of a model village development including almshouses and a children's home. Mrs Pickering performed the opening ceremony, unlocking the wrought-iron gates with a gold key.

Having co-founded Pickering and Haldane's Steam Trawling Co., Pickering would go on to make numerous charitable donations to the people of Hull, with ornamental and sensory gardens, aviaries, and a playground and paddling pool. The Museum of Fisheries and Shipping opened in Pickering Park in 1912 after Thomas Sheppard had obtained a building in Pickering Park from a local trawler owner. It later moved to the Town Docks Museum building in 1974, where it is now known as the Maritime Museum. The associated almshouses, the former museum and a related pumping station, are all listed buildings, as are the original iron park gates, which are one of the few early 20th century ornamental iron structures in Hull to have survived the Second World War drive for scrap iron. The lake is popular for fishing, feeding the geese and ducks and boating in summer.

Left and below: These two photographs, look as they could be from around the time of the opening of Queens Gardens in the centre of Hull. Queen's Dock was purchased from the North Eastern Railway Company by Hull Corporation in 1930 for the sum of £117,000. The dock was subsequently filled in, with Queen's Gardens opening on 19 September, 1935. Having become an obstruction to traffic, the statue of William Wilberforce, atop a 90 foot tall doric column, was re-sited from Queen Victoria Square to its current location at the garden's eastern end. The gardens have a central avenue of trees aligned with the Wilberforce Monument to the east, which is fronted by a pool with

fountains. On the north side of the Gardens a plaque commemorates Robinson Crusoe, the famous fictional character who sailed from Hull in 1651 on the voyage that ended with him castaway on a desert island for over 28 years. The gardens were remodelled between 1959 and 1961, with Frederick Gibberd, a prominent post-war civic designer and architect of Liverpool Metropolitan Cathedral, appointed as consultant. Gibberd would also design the Hull College building close by.

Above: In a predominantly male dominated environment, it was good for the ladies of Hull City Police to strike out on their own and achieve sporting greatness. Slightly overstated maybe, but this group of 21 female bowlers had successfully plundered three trophies in 1956, when this photograph was taken. The English Bowling Association was founded in 1903 and it is very well organised sport which hosts numerous competitions from the club to the national level. Certainly the most famous story in lawn bowls is with Sir Frances Drake and the Spanish Armada. On July 18, 1588, Drake was involved in a game at Plymouth Hoe when he was notified that the Spanish Armada were approaching. His immortalised response was that "We still have time to finish the game and to thrash the Spaniards, too."

Below: This rather bizarre looking bunch of male entertainers are part of the Hull Police Prize taken in 1920. We believe the band was originally founded in 1861, which would potentially make it the oldest continuous police band in the world.

The band celebrated their 150th anniversary in 2011. In this picture we can see the band have stopped to pose for a photograph outside the Lion Clothing Company Pioneer Works in Goulton Street. The general theme of the clothing seems to be scary clown outfits, however we do have one lone Scotsman, together with traditional kilt and sporran. The procession could be linked to Hull's annual fair, which after the First World War became the biggest in the country. The event could also coincide with The Rotary Club of Hull which was chartered on May 1, 1920, and is therefore one of the oldest in the UK.

Women and children line the cobbled streets in Hull, as Versatile Bob and his Boulevard Club's Ragtime Band belt out a tune in front of the supporter's club coach, prior to the Challenge Cup Final against Wigan in 1959. The sign on the front of the coach looks to be 'Up the Francis Boys Hull', most likely in reference to Roy Francis, the first Black British professional coach in any sport, who was coach of the Airlie Birds at the time. After playing his last game on Boxing Day 1955, he switched to coaching, a field in which he was to make an even greater impact. Renowned for his innovative coaching methods, he was regarded as a visionary, leading Hull to title success before going on to win the Challenge Cup with Leeds. He was the first coach to embrace players' families and offer them transport to games. He broke further ground by moving on to coach in Australia with the North Sydney Bears before another brief stint at Leeds, and then Bradford Northern.

Right: For much of the 20th century, the Moores family operated a number of highly profitable businesses under the 'Littlewoods' name, including football pools and mail-order catalogues. The most visible aspect of their lucrative empire, however, was the chain of Littlewoods high street stores. Commercially, they never inspired the same affection as Woolworth. Yet Littlewoods was a strong presence in British shopping centres for a good 65 years, and its closure in 2002 seemed to mark the passing of a retail era. Littlewoods stores were similar to British Home Stores (BHS), selling a variety of low-cost (3d. to 2s. 11d.) clothing and household goods. Food departments were introduced into Littlewoods stores after the war, and as soon as it became feasible the company resumed its expansion policy. By the time of these photographs there were 55 stores open in the UK. These pictures are from the opening of the latest store, in Hull, on 25 November, 1955. Local crowds had come out in force to grab an opening bargain, despite the cold weather. The store, on Whitefriargate, was opened to the public by Lord Mayor, Alderman Fox JP.

Above: Before the construction of the Humber Bridge, Victoria Pier was the main terminal for ferries to depart from here to Lincolnshire. The Pier opened in 1847 and was initially known as Corporation Pier. It was used as the terminus of the Hull to New Holland ferry, the only way to avoid the 60 mile road trip via Goole. It was renamed Victoria Pier, as it is now known today, in 1854, when Queen Victoria left the city from this port following her visit to Hull. A railway booking office latterly named Hull Victoria Pier was established here in 1849 by the Manchester, Sheffield and Lincolnshire Railway (MS&LR). Steamer sisters Wingfield Castle and Tattershall Castle, built in 1934, proved to be essential transporters throughout that period. The service was continued by British Railways in 1965, but ended with the opening of the Humber Bridge in June 1981. In this photograph taken in the mid 1940s, people on the pier are taking an all too rare peaceful moment to watch the steamers pass by.

Left: These young women were having real fun in the mid 30s. Women no longer accepted their position as second class citizens. They threw off the yoke with which men had restrained them and they also abandoned the old, dowdy fashions that restricted freedom both of movement and spirit. In the 1920s, black, floor length dresses were discarded in favour of the short skirts and bright tops of the flapper generation. On the beach, these lovelies laughed at the thought of their grandparents' bathing machines and ankle length costumes. They romped across the sands in daring designs that showed acres of flesh and shocked the conservative element. The women also embraced the League for Health and Beauty. This organisation was founded in 1930 by Mary Bagot Stack with the aim of giving women the opportunity to enjoy physical fitness via a series of programmed exercises.

This is a great action shot from the game between Hull City and West Ham United from the old Division 2 on 12 November, 1955. Pictured 3rd from the left, is the great Stan Mortensen, who spent two seasons with Hull in the mid-1950s. Despite winning the game 3-1, it was not a great season for the 'Tigers' as they were relegated to Division 3. Incredibly though, over 24,000 fans packed into Boothferry Park to watch the game. The opposition that day, included no less than 5 players who would go on to become household names as football managers. In the West Ham line-up were; John Bond, Noel Cantwell, Malcolm Allison, Frank O'Farrell and Dave Sexton. Perhaps Hulls biggest achievement that year was beating Hungarian club side Vasas, in an era when their national team were regarded as the greatest in the world. Hull had stepped in to play at the last minute against the unbeaten tourists and were expected by the media to get thrashed. In what would prove to become a historic game, on Monday, 17 October, 1955, a remarkable hat-trick by Bill Bradbury, who had joined the club from Birmingham that month, saw Hull achieve a famous 3-1 victory.

I n this photograph, radio and television star Terry Thomas drops in on an Ideal exhibition stand at the time of the Festival of Britain in 1951. With his cheeky grin and trademark cigarette-holder, the sight of Thomas has obviously raised a smile or two, apart from the chap at the back, and you can just imagine him saying: "Jolly good show chaps". One of Britain's most beloved eccentric comedians he had just written and starred in a series on the BBC Television Service, How Do You View?, noted for being the first comedy series on British television. He is being shown the very latest 'Classic Boiler' from Ideal Standard (the new name from 1953) who have a long history in Hull dating back to 1906, when the American owned National Radiator Company set up a new factory employing 800 people. The promotion obviously worked, as today Ideal Standard International is a privately held multinational bathroom, sanitary ware and plumbing fixture company headquartered in Belgium.

Local 'girls about town' Jeanne Stather (22) and her friend Jennifer Fussey (19) enjoy lunchtime chips from the open-air stall at Hull market in March 1965. The girls are probably stocking up on carbohydrates, ready for a hectic weekends drinking and dancing. Keeping up with the latest fashion trends, they both had short cut bleach blonde hairstyles. They probably worked near to the market and were happy to pose for a photograph outside Carver's Saloon. Carver's are well known in Hull and recently celebrated 125 years in business. They built a reputation with a stall on Hull market before taking their current premises in Trinity House Lane 37 years ago. Bob Carver's pattie recipe has been a closely guarded secret enjoyed by residents and visitors alike. The origins of the pattie remain a subject of often fierce debate, but the business has been producing them since day one of the business in 1888.

The seaside town of Hornsea is perfect for a family day out, with a lovely sandy beach, a busy promenade to stroll along, amusements and plenty of attractions for all the family. The town has retained a pleasant village atmosphere and it is only 20 miles from the centre of Hull. In this photograph we can see a group of children enjoying a seaside canter on the ponies despite the inclement weather at Hornsea in 1977. Robert Jackson the pony ride owner would take the children for a ride on the beach despite the blustery conditions, as the youngsters still had a great time. The photographer was having quite a difficult time as well, coping with the conditions and getting all the children and ponies in shot. One has already gone rogue and set off towards the sea.

ON THE MOVE IN HULL

Blackburn Aircraft (Blackies), Brough, holds a special place in the hearts of many Hull and East Riding families. Succeeding generations have worked there over the past 100 years. This superbly nostalgic photograph takes us right back to the beginning in 1909. The Blackburn First Monoplane (also known as Monoplane No 1) was a British experimental aircraft constructed by Robert Blackburn. Here we can see his design, complete with garden seat, ready for testing. When complete, it was transported to the beach between Saltburn and Marske for testing from April, 1909. In that year, only taxying trials with the occasional hop were made. The only actual flight, on 24 May, 1910, lasted for around one minute, and unfortunately ended in a crash in which the aircraft was damaged beyond repair.

Above: Day trippers from the Recreation Club at the Belgian Arms in Osborne Street, Hull, pose for a photograph before setting off on their journey. The mixed group are all dressed in their Sunday best for the outing. The date of the trip was 12 August, 1923. The driver was also very smart in his white coat, peaked cap and dickie bow. The coach or charabancs were pretty basic vehicles; noisy, uncomfortable and often poorly upholstered with low-backed seats and used mainly for short journeys to the nearest resort town or the races. Charra's were normally open top, with a large canvas folding hood stowed at the rear in case of rain, much like a convertible motor car. If rain started, this had to be pulled into position, a very heavy task. They offered little or no protection to the passengers in the event of an overturning accident, which contributed to their early demise.

Right: We can see from the clock in the bridge, that it is exactly midday, as this woman crosses the busy road in the centre of Hull. Her style is typical of the 1920s, with a big winter wrap-around coat and a close fitting cloche hat. However, she seems oblivious to the oncoming Hedon Road tram behind her. Back in the 1920s, many of Hull's streets were criss-crossed with tram lines, forming the city's first modern transport system. The Kingston upon Hull tramway network followed the five main roads radially out of the city centre. It is interesting to see that at this time, all the trams carried a route letter rather than number, at each end of the car. This was a normal scene on the roads, as the public randomly crossed the roads in front of cars, trams and single-decker buses.

There are some very nice cars parked outside the Station Hotel (now The Royal Hotel) when this photograph was taken around 60 years ago; a Daimler and a Jaguar, to name but two. The exterior façade of the hotel has changed very little during that time, although the vehicles obviously have. The hotel was completed in 1849, three years after the adjacent Paragon railway station. It catered for all the weary travellers needs and in fact was so well regarded at that time that Queen Victoria and the royal party stayed there in 1853, on a visit to Hull. This picture captures a snapshot of transport at that time, with an array of cars, Corporation buses, taxis, a tankers and even a man on a bicycle. It is interesting that traffic coming along Ferensway, towards the camera, is turning right into Paragon Street, which would be impossible today. The area around the Cenotaph has been pedestrianised and not accessible to vehicles.

English aviator and local heroin, Amy Johnson, arrives at Hedon Airport, near Hull, in her De Havilland DH.60 Gipsy Moth aircraft, nicknamed 'Jason', during celebrations to mark her historic solo flight from London to Darwin in May 1930. Amy set out from Croydon on Monday 5 May, 1930, and arrived in Darwin Australia after a journey that had taken 19 and a half days. She had endured all that the weather could throw at her, monsoon rains, tremendous heat, and desert sandstorms. Although she did not break the record she did attract considerable media attention and was awarded the CBE in the King's birthday honours list. Amy never forgot her home town and in 1932 "The Amy Johnson Cup for Courage" was presented to the City of Hull. The cup was paid for with a purse of sovereigns Amy received from school children in Sydney and was to be awarded each year to a Hull child (under the age of 17) for a deed of courage. Sadly, Amy met an untimely death on 5 January, 1941; she drowned when the plane she was flying crashed into the Thames Estuary during rough weather.

This is a rather poignant photograph outside the Rialto Cinema in Beverley Road, as the ill-fated R38 Airship passes overhead on 21 June, 1921. The ship had been completed at the Shorts factory in Bedfordshire, two weeks earlier and it was heading to Howden, where a detachment of US Navy personnel were waiting. At its peak at the end of World War I, Howden was the biggest airbase in the UK. The giant R38 measured 695ft long and 85ft high and was to be put through its paces at Howden. On 24 August, 1921, after an aborted flight to Pulham in Norfolk, the captain decided to return to Howden and carry out more tests on the way.

While over the Humber, high-speed turns were tried. The stress on the fuselage was too much and the craft broke in two, causing a large explosion, which blew out windows in Hull. Thousands of people watched as it crashed in flames into the Humber, just off Victoria Pier. Of the crew of 49, only five survived. The Rialto Cinema in Beverley Road, was originally opened as the Coliseum. Adjacent to Stepney Railway Station, the original cinema was converted from part of the Beverley Road skating rink in Terry Street and opened on 9 December, 1912. It changed its name to the Rialto in 1920, later becoming the 'National', taking its name from the National Picture Theatre which had been gutted by fire during the Hull Blitz. The 'National' was converted into a bowling alley in 1961 and burnt down in 1974.

How's this for an unusual motorised contraption. A Northern Dairies girl is out on the streets of Hull delivering milk in the 1930s, driving a three wheeled perambulator. The introduction of the milk bottle altered the appearance of the perambulators as they acquired a 'roof' often with a frame to hold additional crates. Milkmen and in this case milkwomen, were an integral part of everyday life in the UK and in the late Sixties and Seventies it is estimated that they delivered to around 99 per cent of households. They were a vital service to our communities and by nature are cheerful, helpful people. A number of celebrities have been milkmen — including Sixties pop star Freddie Garrity of Freddie And The Dreamers, who drove his band to a BBC audition in Manchester in his milk-cart. Crooner Matt Munro also worked as a milkman, as did James Bond actor Sean Connery. He wasn't the only 007 who did a milk round: Roger Moore was a milkman's lad as a teenager in Stockwell, South London. My favourite was 'Ernie' who drove the fastest milk cart in the west.

Above: In this photograph the transport in question, is more about manoeuvring the heavy load from A to B without dropping it on the dockside. The Albert Dock had all the heavy duty lifting gear required to get the job done, as we can see in this image from September 1951. Smaller items of cargo were handballed from the back of lorries, but this railway locomotive engine was a completely different kettle of fish. So much so, that a small crowd had gathered on the quayside to watch the events unfold. In the background is a rare view of the Riverside Quay Clock Tower, which was sadly demolished later in the decade.

Left: It's not clear what health and safety rules are in operation here, as this group of men help to position this out of service tram on St Andrews Dock in 1954. The very delicate lifting operation is well under way as the No45 tram is loaded on to a cargo for pastures new. We can only assume the process was successful, despite the flimsy looking chains holding the tram in place. This particular tram must have been out of commission for almost ten years by the time this photograph was taken. Hopefully, it is not going to meet its maker, but instead on to a transport museum or even perhaps to be used in service in another country.

By the 1950s the UK was the second-largest manufacturer of cars in the world (after the United States) and the largest exporter. This was good news for the dock workers as there was a steady flow of vehicles for export, many for the American market, leaving the port of Hull. This photograph from September 1950, shows cars being hoisted by heavy duty cranes on to the transport ships moored at the King George's dockside. The very stylish two-tone Hillman Minx MkV convertible made for the export market can be seen with left hand drive. The King George Dock was the last of the ten Hull docks to be opened, when ships began using it in 1914.

Below: This is one of East Yorkshire Motor Service buses, prior to departure on route to Birmingham in 1934. The Leyland 'Tiger' single-decker coaches were used on a network of express routes – known as Yorkshire Services, which operated from a depot at Anlaby Road. By the 1930s the charabanc had evolved into a more comfortable form of transport: the motor coach. These more comfortable express bus services offered speedy travel around Britain, including destinations like Birmingham and London. Coupled with the growth in availability of cars, these new forms of transport, led to more far-flung days out. Maybe in reality it was not that speedy, as in the 1930 Transport Act coaches were subject to a 30mph speed limit.

Right: In this photograph we can see the majestic and imposing presence of the 'Pommern' at the docks in Hull in 1934. The Pommern, formerly the Mneme (1903–1908), is a windjammer. It is a four-masted barque that was built in 1903 in Glasgow, Scotland at the J. Reid & Co shipyard. This huge container ship, was one of the Flying P-Liners, the famous sailing ships of the German shipping company F. Laeisz. Later she was acquired by Gustaf Erikson of Mariehamn in the Finnish Åland archipelago, who used her to carry grain from the Spencer Gulf area in Australia to harbours in England or Ireland until the start of World War II. After World War II, Pommern was donated to the town of Mariehamn as a museum ship. Pommern has the reputation of being a "lucky ship". She survived both world wars unscathed, lost only four crew members at sea on her journeys, and won the Great Grain Races twice, 1930 and 1937. From 1923 it sailed under the Finnish flag, making a final journey from Hull to Mariehamn in 1939.

There is an interesting mix of vehicles in this photograph from the mid-1950s. George Street with no road markings, looks much wider than it does today with its traffic regulations and wide pavements. The Morris Minor and Ford Anglia E494A (later to become Ford Popular) in the foreground, are classic vehicles from the time. Poet Philip Larkin described Hull as 'very nice and flat for cycling' – and in the 1950s a third of the population rode regularly, and we can get a feel for that from this picture. According to Hull's Streetlife Museum, 100,000 people in the city still rode regularly in the early 1950s. The streets would have clattered and rung with the din of thousands of boneshakers as workers streamed to and from factories, docks and building sites. The elegant building on the right, is still recognisable today. At that time it was the home of Hull Young Peoples' Christian and Literary Institution, originally founded in 1860.

This is an unusual sight from the docks in Hull, as we can see hundreds of Morris Minor vehicles lined up; probably for export. The Morris Minor is a British car that debued at the Earls Court Motor Show, London, on 20 September, 1948. Designed under the leadership of Alec Issigonis, more than 1.3 million were manufactured between 1948 and 1972 in three series and is considered a classic example of automotive design, as well as typifying 'Englishness'. By 1950, most 'Minors' were exported in the drive to 'export or die', and around 75 percent of early production found its way overseas and one major market was America. Only ten years later, on December 22, 1960, a milestone in the history of the Morris Minor was achieved; the millionth car rolled of the production line at Cowley.

This photograph from October, 1965, features the unmistakable smooth lines of Sir Donald Campbell's Bluebird. The cockpit cover was propped up and a mirror positioned to allow enthusiasts to glimpse the controls. The car on display at Kennings Analby Road showroom, was the original car used to set the land speed record by the irrepressible British hero. In an age in which it seemed Britain could still lead the world, Donald Campbell stood head and shoulders above almost everyone. It is sad to remember that only two years after this photograph was taken, he was to lose his life in another record attempt, this time on water.

These three giraffes might be a bit surprised to find themselves on the docks in Hull. They have been unloaded from the North Sea Ferries, Norwave (built in 1966) seen in the background, in transit to Chester Zoo in 1970. North Sea Ferries was a joint Anglo-Dutch company, of which the Dutch half was owned by Nordzee Veerdiensten of Rotterdam, which is where these giraffes were last on dry land. In the 1960s and 1970s there was a growing unease about how animals were treated in captivity, so certain campaign groups may not have been too happy about these animals living prospects in the zoo. For the family's who enjoy a day out visiting the zoo, they were a great addition to the menagerie of animals on show. Because of their height these giraffes are being transported in specially built crates and are able to get a giraffes-eye view of the docks. One of the giraffes on a previous transportation in 1959, was George, who was thought to be the world's tallest giraffe in captivity an amazing 19ft 3in tall (5.88 meters).

Left: It is 80 years since the official opening of Hulls trolleybus system on Friday 23 July, 1937, which gradually replaced the tramway network. This photograph from the mid-1950s shows a fine example of Hull's distinctively liveried Sunbeam MF2B Coronation type trolleybus, turning left on to Spring Bank. The trolleybus No62 was making its way along Princes Avenue from the terminus at the junction of Cottingham Road and Newlands Avenue. At its peak, the Hull system had a total of 7 routes and a maximum fleet of 100 trolleybuses. The most unusual sight in this picture is to see a woman in flowery summer dress and hat driving on the main road. The 50cc Honda Moped she was riding could still be dangerous, particularly without a crash helmet which didn't become compulsory in the UK until 1973.

Right: Everybody in Hull knows of Jackson's, having worked for them or been a customer. William Jackson opened his first shop in Scale Lane in Hull's old town in 1851, later moving to Carr Lane. On the back of this spectacular growth, the company decided to develop its food production capacity and moved its operations to the present site off Derringham Street. By the 1930s, the business had grown to fifty-plus shops. To supply these shops, the firm needed a reliable fleet of vehicles. Here in this photograph, probably from the late 1940s, we can see the impressive row of Austin vans waiting to collect their delivery loads, outside the old Victoria Street Factory. By this time, there were almost 100 shops to service, scattered throughout most of Yorkshire.

Right: A lone car park attendant oversees the comings and goings at the small Hammonds car park along Ferensway in Hull. According to the iconic Guinness sign in the distance, we can see the photograph was taken at 3.30pm. A variety of the latest motorcars of the period add a touch of nostalgia to the scene. Cars from manufacturers such as Morris, Ford, Austin and Hillman are on display. We know the photograph was

taken at the end of July 1966, so its interesting to speculate as to the actual day. It could be it was the same day England were winning the World Cup Final at Wembley, on 30 July, in front of 93,000 spectators, with another 400 million people around the world watching the match on television. This means little to this conscientious car park attendant who will continue to do his job regardless.

Below: There are very few people out on the street when this photograph was taken back in 1959. At first glance this could be the main street of any number of sleepy market towns in the heart of rural England. The individual shops and jolly awnings, bring back memories of a more peaceful and less frenetic age. Yet this was no Grantchester, but Hessle Square on a hot summers day. Perhaps the give away in this picture is the double-decker, with a very individual and almost unique gothic style roof. This roof profiling was used on most East Yorkshire buses at the time. When going on the top deck, the overall effect was of entering a gothic church, with a definite arching of the roofline with mid-blue painted window frames.

The best example of the need for such an unusual shape, is perfectly illustrated in the accompanying photograph, as a light coloured bus carefully squeezes through the arch at Beverley Bar, on the way to Leeds.

We can see clearly from the clock on Holy Trinity Church that it is 2.43pm when this photograph was taken. A lone Rover car is passing the famous King Billy statue in Market Place. The photographer must be standing outside what is now Hull Magistrates Court, looking across towards Holy Trinity Church.

The impressive statue is of King William III (William of Orange), was paid for by public subscription in 1734. Hull was the first large city in Britain to swear their allegiance to the new King when he deposed James II in 1685. King Billy's presence over the ornate Victorian public conveniences speaks volumes of his status as more 'great reliever' than 'great deliverer'. Around 1880, a plain drinking fountain was added below the inscription and in the late 1800's the four lamps were added at the corners of the plinth. These were made by local firm King and Peach. It was the only piece of public art in Hull to removed to safety for the Second World War, when it was taken to Sancton near Market Weighton. It was reinstated in 1948.

Standing in the shadow of the famous King Billy statue, it is one of Hull's most historic pubs. There are several myths surrounding the statue, one of which is that when the clock of Holy Trinity strikes midnight, King Billy gets off his horse and goes for a drink in the nearby King William pub.

Holy Trinity Church is an Anglican parish church. It is the largest parish church in England by floor area. The church dates back to about 1300 and contains what is widely acknowledged to be some of the finest mediaeval brick-work in the country. On 7 November, 2016, Archbishop of York John Sentamu announced that the Grade 1 listed church would be given Minster status during the City of Culture year.

Above: This is a photograph of the historic North Bar in Beverley. Beverley Bar or North Bar is a 15th-century gate, located on Lairgate, close to Beverley Minster and abuts buildings on either side. The bars also acted as toll gates, passage through them having to be paid for as a sort of local tax. There are records of the North Bar being used as viewing gallery for the town governors in the 15th and 16th centuries during the plays that occurred at the Corpus Christi festivals. On the South face above the centre point of the arch is some protruding brickwork of three shields hanging from a line. It is designated a Grade I listed building and is now recorded in the National Heritage List for England. Traffic is limited to single file through the bar arch and controlled by a set of lights. The photograph was taken from in front of the Rose & Crown public house.

Right: The weather in Hull was miserable when this photograph was taken at 9.35am outside Paragon Station in 1937. The 'Holiday Handbook' provided the right ingredients to escape from the drudgery of daily life. The LNER company had the answer to our summertime blues, even though it would be another 20 years until Eddie Cochran sang about it for the first time. This book, 'The herald of

the holiday season', was available for potential sun seekers for a mere 6d and it allowed unlimited travel for a whole week. This was a golden age for rail travel, as families found motor cars too expensive to maintain and run from their meagre wages. Steam locomotives were pushing back the frontiers of speed. The Cheltenham Flyer and the Flying Scotsman set records that approached 100mph. For those not wanting to get away from it all, child star, Shirley Temple, was appearing in her latest movie 'Heidi' at the Regal Cinema.

SUCCESS STORIES

The companies and organisations that have thrived in the area over recent decades, are many. In the next few pages we take great pleasure in including a selection of these companies, which all have a proud history in Hull. Readers may well recognise and even have worked at one of the diverse range of local companies featured. With their co-operation and access to their respective photographic archives, we have been able to tell their stories. Hopefully these interesting and thought provoking features will give a small indication of how these respected Hull companies have impacted on the local community, bringing much needed sustainability and economic prosperity to the area.

Right: Three Scottish fisher girls seen on the quay at Hull fish dock on September 1946, waiting for the fishing fleet to return. The girls would follow the herring fleets around the East Coast, stopping in temporary lodgings while the work was plentiful. After a brisk unloading on the pier from the herring drifters, teams of migrant Scottish girls, hired by the curing firms, set to work gutting, cleaning, sorting and packing the 'silver darlings' into barrels. The work was long and hard, but these girls were so fast they could gut and pack 30-50 herring a minute and this made them a minor tourist attraction. Gutting with sharp knives inevitably resulted in painful cuts and sores, which were constantly aggravated by contact with the salt. The women protected their fingers with "clooties or cloots", crude bandages made from old rags and cotton flour sacks bought cheaply from bakers. These women knitted whenever they had free time, and incorporated patterns they saw in other areas.

For many years Russia produced about a 40 percent of the world's fur and despite the scruffy, uninspiring appearance of the cargo being unloaded in this photograph, it is packed with 95 tons of Russian furs valued at £670,000. The valuable shipment had just arrived at King George's Dock aboard SS Pulkovo, on 1 September, 1960. Security looks fairly relaxed with just one policeman in view, in the background. Once unloaded the furs would have been taken by road to the London sales rooms. Animal rights issues were less prevalent at this time and both male and female Russians traditionally wore furs to keep warm in the long winter months.

H ull is the only city in the UK not served by BT and with its own independent telephone network company, now called Kingston Communications. In the early days of telephony, through roughly the 1960s, companies used manual telephone switchboards, and switchboard operators connected calls by inserting a pair of phone plugs into the appropriate jacks. Before the advent of operator distance dialing and customer Direct Dial (DDD) calling, switchboard operators would work with their counterparts in the distant central office to complete long distance calls. Before the advent of automatic exchanges, an operator's assistance was required for anything other than calling telephones across a shared party line. Callers spoke to an operator at a Central Office who then connected a cord to the proper circuit in order to complete the call. Being in complete control of the call.

Hull Brewery were prolific in their output of beer in bottles and these young ladies can be seen packing the bottles into crates for shipment. The Second World War led to a drop in trade, and many of the company's properties were damaged or destroyed during the Hull Blitz. The Silvester Street brewery, however, remained intact and continued production. Dark mild was the chosen drink of Hull's trawlermen and these girls would have had to pack plenty of crates to keep up with demand. It gushed down thirsty throats in some quantity, particularly during the 1950s and early 1960s. The Star and Garter, otherwise known as Raynor's after a local licensee, stood on the corner of Hessle Road and West Dock Avenue, braced for an invasion soon after the lock gates swung open to admit the first homecoming ship. Apparently, the landlord would ensure that a hundred pints were laid out on the bar before he opened the door.

Above: ABI Summer Breeze offers room, comfort and style. *Below:* The current ABI logo. *Bottom:* ABI started in business producing caravans and moved onto holiday homes.

ABI (UK) Ltd

Providing holiday homes for leisurely living

Holiday homes have been transformed beyond recognition since the Ace Caravan Company was formed in Hull back in 1962 to manufacture touring caravans.

The business has evolved through the years and the company, now known as ABI, is a market leader in luxurious holiday homes which are enjoyed by families across the UK and Europe.

The reputation of ABI, based at Beverley, East Yorkshire, was initially built on its range of touring caravans manufactured to the highest standards, and that attention to quality has remained a mainstay of the company as it developed state-of-the art products which are manufactured locally.

Over 450 people are employed by the company and the skills and knowledge gained over the decades are now put to excellent use manufacturing high specification holiday homes and lodges.

ABI is the second largest supplier into the UK market by volume and supplies all of the major holiday park groups, as well as smaller groups, independent parks and dealerships.

110

The Humberside region has a long history of manufacturing caravans and relocatable buildings and there are several theories as to why that should be.

Some believe the industry grew from being close to a major port that imported timber and sheet materials. Others think that staff from some of the earliest established manufacturers left to set up their own successful businesses.

But, there is no doubt that Hull, as an excellent port from which to export to Europe, is an ideal location and why the biggest manufacturers of holiday homes and touring caravans have made their base in the area.

*Above: An aerial photograph of the ABI site at Beverley. **Inset:** A family in the 1960s enjoying the freedom a holiday home offers.*

In the early 1960s the Ace Caravan Company started producing tourers with boat shaped roofs and in 1963 showcased them at the Caravan Exhibition in London at prices ranging from £279 to £405.

Around the same time another company called Belmont Caravans Ltd began making caravan holiday homes in the same area as Ace. Both companies were successful and became market leaders in their fields and by 1970 were manufacturing their own models on adjoining sites in Beverley. Then, in 1972, the two companies merged to form Ace Belmont International. There was

a management buyout of ABI in 1988 to form ABI Leisure Group Ltd and the decision was taken to float the company on the London Stock Exchange to raise equity to fund future developments. At that time the company was valued at over £33 million.

ABI was already established internationally and exports accounted for a significant proportion of turnover. The business had benefited from families at home and abroad becoming more mobile and willing to travel further afield for holidays. Then, the opening of the channel tunnel again increased the numbers travelling between the UK and Europe.

Business partnerships with distributors were also flourishing and in the mid-1990s ABI was exporting more than 80% of the touring caravan exports into the Dutch market. The French and German

111

markets also resulted in successful ventures. A motor caravan manufacturer known as Auto-Trail Ltd had also been acquired to complement the group's other products and in 1994 the Vanroyce brand of luxury touring caravans was also added to the group.

With the importance of the European market and recognition of the need for a top-class after-sales service, language skills were very valuable to the company and it employed bi-lingual and multi-lingual staff throughout its departments in Beverley.

Investment has continued to ensure quality products of the highest integrity are manufactured. This has also involved using state-of-the-art manufacturing equipment and adapting to the needs of the industry.

An example of this was the early boat shaped roofs on tourers which were widely acclaimed at the time but had to be replaced by far more complex and technically superior models. This was in part due to the "green lobby" of the automotive industry which put pressure on car makers to build vehicles with smaller engines which were still able to tow reasonable loads.

Consequently, the next generation caravans were designed to be more aerodynamic and therefore less prone to drag and easier for smaller engined vehicles to tow.

The ongoing challenges over the years have also seen recessions and increasing competition pose difficulties and there were further top-level changes.

Above: An early advertisement for the Belmont range. Below: Comfort and style was as important in the 1960s as it is today.

A decision was taken at the beginning of this century to cease caravan tourer manufacturing and concentrate on the holiday home sector of the business for which management saw more potential – and the business has continued to flourish ever since resulting in a commanding market share of 25%.

Today's products which will provide many years of enjoyment for generations of families, are the result of many years dedication which has helped the business expand its knowledge and expertise and develop technology year-after-year.

Each year improvements are made to enhance holiday homes – the addition of little touches and at the same time creating new ranges – this attention to detail ensures that ABI remains the business that customers old and new are attracted towards.

The 2017 range features 11 impressive holiday homes, different in style but all benefiting from the best craftsmanship. They are known by their names: Summer Breeze, Oakley, Blenheim, Sunningdale, Elan, Derwent, Clarendon, Ambleside, Kingsbourne, Beaumont and Westwood.

The attention to detail is not always visible and obvious, such as extra insulation in the roof or the premium hinges fitted to cupboard doors.

The quality is far superior to what people could have expected just a few years ago and all ABI holiday homes come with enhanced standard features such as 7ft high walls combined with vaulted ceilings; the latest home technologies such as Bluetooth sound

Above: The changing logo of ABI from 1974 - 2000.

systems and USB sockets; low-E thermoglass double glazing which helps keep bills down; and high quality furniture fittings which not only look great but stand the test of time and include extra details such as soft-close drawers.

They are also designed to be environmentally friendly with energy saving light bulbs; water-saving sanitaryware; 50mm fibreglass wall insulation and 100m fibreglass roof insulation. To limit the risk of damp in shower rooms, closed top shower cubicles are fitted to prevent moisture escaping.

Condensing central heating boilers are fitted and impressive kitchens feature externally vented cooker hoods. Domestic quality mattresses, carpets and underlay are fitted as standard.

People today spend more on leisure than ever before and first time holiday-homers are coming into the market every year. ABI works hard to guide them through the buying process and beyond.

Most people will know where in the country they would like their ABI home to be sited so they are then encouraged to explore holiday parks in that area and find the one they want. They are then advised to consider available pitches and the direction their windows face as that can influence which ABI holiday home is bought.

Ultimately the choice of which ABI holiday home will be determined by the size of the pitch and that is why the company manufactures an extensive range of sizes, varying in both width and length for each model. Budgeting should also account for additional costs such as annual site fees, gas, electric and water, TV licence and insurance costs.

Because ABI prides itself on the craftsmanship and attention to detail in all its holiday homes the warranties it offers give unrivalled protection to ensure its customers have peace of mind from day one.

Everything inside an ABI is covered by a 12 months parts and labour guarantee, and there is a further 24 months cover on furniture manufactured and fitted by ABI and a range of accessories such as shower cubicles, radiators, gutters, sockets and the kitchen sink. There is a five year warranty on chassis, roof, walls, ceiling, floors

Above centre: Some of the thousands of screws and brackets used to produce holiday homes for ABI.
Right: A craftsman at work producing the interiors for ABI.

and external windows and doors and a 10 year warranty on fully galvanised chassis.

Every ABI holiday home also benefits from extra space provided by sundecks and unlike ordinary wooden decking there is no need for time consuming and expensive maintenance. Decking used is strong, timber-free boarding on sturdy galvanised steel sub-frames for a long, weather-proof and low maintenance life. The decking can also be co-ordinated to the design chosen with the ideal matching accessories, such as access ramps and built-in lighting, to provide the finishing touch to the exterior of an ABI holiday home.

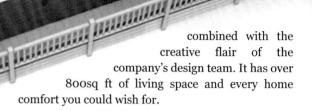

An exciting new development at ABI was the launch of its first holiday lodge – The Harrogate. It was designed to make a statement and be a showstopper and many years of expertise in building holiday homes was harnessed and combined with the creative flair of the company's design team. It has over 800sq ft of living space and every home comfort you could wish for.

The Harrogate luxury lodge is built to residential specification as standard and delivers outstanding style, quality and craftsmanship throughout.

The open-plan living space features spectacular cathedral style windows that flood the room with light and freestanding furniture,

Above: A 3D plan of The Harrogate. Below: The Kingsbourne holiday lodge is full of character and luxurious features.

Above: *A craftsman puts the finishing touches to one of the holiday homes.*

stylish lighting and serene natural tones and rich textures. A large, fully equipped kitchen features high quality appliances. The spacious bedrooms with full sized double and single beds also provide plenty of storage space.

The holiday homes may be static but ABI has never stood still throughout its history as it has continually pushed the boundaries in quality and design to ensure it remains at the forefront of its industry, successfully delivering holiday homes for generations of families to spend quality time together in their "home from

home." There is an extensive UK and European dealership network and more information is available on the company website www. abiuk.co.uk

Right: *Relax in comfort in the ABI Beaumont.*

Andrew Marr International
Navigating the way to success

With a well established heritage and history that stretches back over a hundred years, the Marr name is synonymous with development and innovation within the seafood industry.

The group, which is based in Hessle, is involved in a broad range of marine and shore-based activities including seafood trading and marketing, fishing vessel investment and management, temperature controlled storage and food manufacturing.

In 2008, when the Hull company J Marr (Seafoods) Ltd received the Queen's Award for Enterprise for the second time, it was undoubtedly a feather in the cap for this well-known local business. The company is a wholly owned subsidiary of Andrew Marr International Limited, which has around 270 employees and an annual turnover in excess of £500 million.

By the opening years of the new millennium, J Marr (Seafoods) Ltd, a wholly-owned subsidiary of Andrew Marr International,

*Above: Company founder, Joseph Marr. **Below:** The J Marr & Son Limited fish landing staff, circa 1920s.*

had become a world renowned fish trading company specialising in the sourcing, shipment and sale of frozen 'pelagic' - that is to say, mid water - fish harvested from the Atlantic and Pacific Oceans and shipped to markets in West Africa, Eastern Europe, and the Middle and Far East. Andrew Marr International was formed in 1986 following a de-merger of the far older Hull-based business of J Marr & Son Limited.

The story of the Marr family in Hull really begins in 1860, when 25 year old Joseph Marr, the son of a seafarer who had sailed in Hull's whaling fleet and died in Greenland, rented two smoking-kilns in the Dairycoates district of Hull. Joseph started up in business for himself as a fish curer, a trade he had learned from his stepfather. Soon afterwards Joseph was able to buy his own curing houses, and in 1870, extending his operations, he became the owner of a newly built fishing smack, the Adelaide. Business prospered: during the fifteen years which followed his purchase of the Adelaide Joseph bought a further six vessels, all of them newly built.

These were boom years for Hull. By 1887 no fewer than 448 smacks were fishing from the port. In 1891, Joseph, now joined by his son James, ordered his first steam trawler. The last two of Marr's sail-powered smacks were sold in 1902. Less than a year later, steam had completely replaced all of Hull's fishing smacks.

In 1898 James Marr had moved to Fleetwood with several key employees taking a fleet of three steam trawlers.

The founder of the business, Joseph Marr, died in 1900. As a consequence, in 1902, the firm became a limited company, J Marr & Son Limited, with James Marr as its first Chairman.

The focus now shifted completely to Fleetwood,

where, by 1913, the company fleet consisted of 32 trawlers with 11 more on order. The outbreak of the First World War, however seriously disrupted operations, with both trawlers and their crews being called up. Tragically, in 1916 James Marr died at the age of 47, leaving the future of the business in serious jeopardy.

At the time of James's death his son, Alan Marr, was overseas, serving in a Fleetwood Pals battalion. Alan was not able to return and take over operations until 1919, only a year before the last of the Marr trawlers finally returned from war service.

Very sadly, Alan Marr would live for only another six years and on his death in 1925, the reins of the company would pass to Alan's 20-year twin brothers, Leslie and Geoffrey Marr, who in 1934 moved the company back to Hull after an absence of 36 years, though continuing to also run trawlers out of Fleetwood.

In September 1939, when war with Germany broke out once again, the company was one of the first to suffer its effects. Two of Marr's Fleetwood-based trawlers, Arlita and Minto, were sunk by German gunfire, their crews having first been transferred to the Nancy Hague which was then ordered by the German navy to return to port. By 1940, the company's entire fleet, with the exception of two small trawlers, had either been sunk or requisitioned for war service.

The war inevitably led to a suspension of the fishing industry, and the company's offices on St Andrew's Dock in Hull were closed. Later, during a heavy air raid in 1941, the premises completely disappeared after a German landmine destroyed a large part of the northern end of the dock.

When hostilities finally ceased, in 1945, the once mighty Marr fleet would consist of just six small trawlers.

New trawlers were however soon commissioned and the fleet began to grow once more. Meanwhile Marr's on-shore operations continued to progress, and in 1957 the company acquired the old established fish importing and exporting business of Andrew Johnson Knudtzon Limited. With that company came a 6,000 ton capacity public cold store - one of the largest in the North of England.

By now J Marr & Son Limited had become a major undertaking and was recognised as the largest privately owned business in the British fish trade. Geoffrey and Leslie Marr's ambition had been

to establish a network of companies handling all aspects of the fish trade - everything from catching, landing and processing to distribution: the company even owned several fish and chip shops!

All was not well however with the fishing industry: the first Cod War erupted in 1957, when Iceland extended its fishing limits to 12 miles, making it necessary for British trawlers, harassed by Icelandic gunboats, to fish under the protection of the Royal Navy.

Top: St Andrew's Dock full of trawlers during the trawler crews' strike in 1935. Left: The three sons of James Herbert Marr circa 1924, left to right: Alan Marr, Geoffrey Edwards Marr and Leslie James Marr. Below: The trial run of the Clevela in 1930, on board are Geoffrey Edwards Marr, Charles Towne, George Everingham, Edward Towne, Henry Atkinson and Percy Edwards.

first vessel of her kind in the world able to freeze her entire catch and able to handle 25 tonnes of fish a day on her newly designed vertical plate freezers. In addition there were facilities aboard the Junella for blast freezing large fish such as halibut and a storage capacity for up to 300 tonnes. A further nine more freezer stern trawlers would be built for the company over the following 13 years.

Sadly, Leslie Marr died in 1963, having made a major contribution to the re-establishment of the family company in Hull in the early post-war years. He had also been the instigator of Marr's impressive post-war shipbuilding programme. His son, Andrew Leslie Marr, was appointed to the board following his father's death.

Geoffrey Edwards Marr died in February 1969 at the age of 64. He had been a director of the company for 44 years and Chairman for 40.

During his tenure he had guided the company successfully through the slump of the 1930s and the devastation of WWII - challenges which had led to the demise of so many competitors. By acquiring ancillary companies and developing the fishing fleet he and his twin brother Leslie had made J Marr & Son Limited the largest privately owned fishing company in Britain. In March 1969, Geoffrey Alan Marr succeeded his father as Chairman. During the 1960s and 1970s a new management team demonstrated the company's faith in the future of the distant water fishing industry by embarking on a multi-million pound shipbuilding programme. In 1967, J.Marr & Son Limited acquired Peter & J. Johnstone Ltd in Aberdeen. By the late 1970s a total of 21 vessels were built.

Above: The Thornella H84 laid up for survey and repairs in the 1960s. The picture was taken from the Company's office window. Right: Emptying the codend aboard the Swanella H141 in April 1960.

Andrew Leslie Marr, Leslie's son, joined J Marr & Son in 1959 as a trainee at a time when the company was developing its freezing-at-sea project: this would be an enormous leap forward for the distant water sector of the fishing industry. At that time fish, stored in crushed ice, could only be kept for around 15 days before they began to deteriorate, thus limiting the time that could be spent at sea. Initially a pilot freezing plant was installed under the whaleback of the Marbella; later a small freezing compartment and low temperature store was built into the hold of the Junella. Andrew Marr sailed with skipper Syd Morrell on the Junella to gain an insight into these experiments: during the first few days of fishing, some 3,000 stones of fish were deep frozen, whilst the rest of the catch filled the hold in the traditional manner.

In 1962, a new Junella, H347, was launched: she was 240 ft. long, grossed 1,435 tons and cost £350,000. The new Junella was the

By the mid-1970s the company was operating eight large freezer trawlers fishing in the North Atlantic. Catches were processed and distributed all around the UK via a chain of depots operated by J Marr Fish Merchants Limited which had become a flourishing business in its own right.

Storm clouds gathered on the horizon however as 200 mile fishing limits became established around the world. British trawlers were denied access to the rich Icelandic fishing grounds

Above: *Andrew Johnson Knudtzon's offices and cold storage premises on the Boulevard, Hull.* **Right:** *The freezer stern trawler Junella H347 arrives at her home port of Hull in July 1962.*

in 1976: resulting in many trawler owning companies going out of business. For J Marr & Son Limited however this was not the end of the business, merely the end of an era, but long term survival depended on diversification.

Alan and Andrew Marr, made the decision to convert some of their freeze trawlers to catch herring and mackerel in UK waters. Other vessels were converted to undertake seismic survey work in the North Sea when offshore oil exploration was gathering pace.

J Marr & Son Limited soon had several of its wet fish trawlers engaged in mackerel fishing and several other vessels operating through Peter and J Johnstone Limited, which had become a prominent fish selling business in the North East of Scotland.

A new subsidiary, J Marr (Seafoods) Limited, was established in 1976 to develop what would eventually become a flourishing business exporting frozen pelagic fish to West Africa, Russia and the Far East.

But what of the long term future? In the early 1980s Andrew Marr and his cousin Alan, who had five sons between them, felt that they should address the issue of succession and a de-merger took place in April 1986. J Marr & Son Limited was restructured into two companies and its assets shared between Andrew and Alan Marr's families.

Following the de-merger the activities of the business which now became Andrew Marr International comprised J Marr (Seafoods), AJK Cold Stores, P&J Johnstone Limited and lastly Marr Frozen Foods which took over the activities

Above: *A fish market scene in Abidjan, Ivory Coast.* **Below left:** *The launch of the MT Northella at Cook Welton & Gemmell Shipyard in 1958.* **Below right:** *The MT Northella in the River Humber; under the command of Skipper Charles Drever, she won The Silver Cod Trophy in 1961.*

of J Marr Fish Merchants. It was agreed that Andrew Marr International Limited would move out of the old offices on St Andrew's Dock and new premises were built at Livingstone Road in Hessle, which were completed in 1989.

The group has however continued to invest in the cold storage business and today Andrew Johnson Knudtzon (AJK) Ltd is the leading northern cold storage provider, with three major locations in the port of Hull.

Andrew Marr Inter-national Limited decided to exit from fish processing in 1988, and Marr Frozen Foods was sold to its management team. About the same time, Andrew Marr International bought a confectionery business in Harrogate – Stanley's Toffee – which subsequently became Food Design Limited, producing high quality confectionery ingredients

for the food manufacturing sector. The Food Design business was sold in 2005.

Andrew Marr International continues to invest in fish catching in the U.K. through its subsidiary Peter & J. Johnstone Ltd which has offices in Peterhead and Fraserburgh. The company has become one of the leading firms of fishing vessel managers and fish salesmen in North-East Scotland. P&J.J also provides expert advice to fishermen on many complex issues concerning licensing and quota management.

J. Marr (Seafoods) Ltd has grown into a highly successful international fish business sourcing pelagic fish around the world and selling in many export core markets, including Africa, Eastern Europe and the Far East, J Marr Seafoods is widely recognised today as a world leader in the fish business and J Marr (Commodities) Ltd are dedicated to providing a similar trade in frozen meat and poultry.

The Fastnet Group was acquired in 2004, has its headquarters in Grimsby and a network of depots in the U.K. The Fastnet name has become synonymous with top quality and has built an international reputation for the supply of sustainable frozen fish and seafood to processors, food service and the fish and chip shop sectors. Its Scottish subsidiary Fastnet Highlands process Langoustines for export to European markets. They are

Top left: *The P&J.J partnership pelagic vessel Christina S.* **Top right:** *P&J.J vessels Castlewood and Attain.* **Centre:** *The firm's Head Office in Hull.* **Left:** *The P&J.J pair trawler, Guiding Star.*

engaged in the sourcing of frozen seafood worldwide for customers in the processing, wholesale and retail sectors.

In 2012 Andrew Marr International established a new business – Marrfish Limited – operating from a depot in Bishop Stortford, to distribute catches of top quality fresh fish caught by P & J J Vessels, to hotels and restaurants in London and the South East.

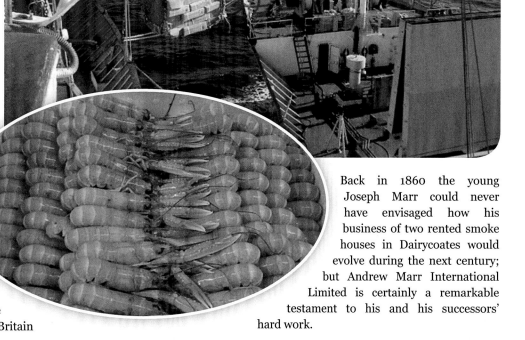

Andrew Marr has three sons in the business: Alexander heads up the Group's fish trading activities and Christian is responsible for the Group's operations in North-East Scotland. Sebastian is a Non-Executive Director. The name of the Marr family has been renowned in the fishing industry for well over a century. Today, in the twenty-first century, the name is more widely known than ever, not just in Britain but all around the world.

Back in 1860 the young Joseph Marr could never have envisaged how his business of two rented smoke houses in Dairycoates would evolve during the next century; but Andrew Marr International Limited is certainly a remarkable testament to his and his successors' hard work.

Above: An example of Fastnet Highlands' high quality production (circled). *Top:* A trans-shipment in the Pacific for J. Marr (Seafoods)' customers (top). *Below:* Andrew Marr with his sons Sebastian, Christian and Alexander.

Above: The Marrfish premises at Bishop Stortford.

With a global footprint and a portfolio of companies across all sectors of the industry, from logistics and sourcing to trading and distribution, they continue to enhance their hard-earned reputation within the seafood and commodities sectors.

Today, with an ongoing commitment to the industry, they are always exploring ways to enhance the business and forge new alliances and partnerships.

BAE Systems
A proud 100 years in the East Riding

Aircraft manufacturing has continued in Brough since 1916 making it one of the oldest sites in the world.

Now, part of the BAE Systems military aircraft business, it employs approximately 950 people with a focus on cutting edge engineering, technology and manufacturing.

BAE Systems is one of the world's largest defence companies with over 83,000 employees spread across the globe, serving customers across the air, land, maritime and national security domains.

The Brough site was founded by Robert Blackburn in 1916 as a sea-plane base, under Blackburn Aeroplane and Motor Company Ltd.

The site was later commandeered by the Government and released back to Blackburn's after the First World War in 1919.

The following year brought a major development which proved a turning point in the company's fortunes. The Air Ministry issued a requirement for a new torpedo-carrying aircraft and Blackburn's collaborated with Napiers. The prototype, called the Swift, was the forerunner of a range of naval bi-planes that established Blackburn's as specialists in the construction of naval aircraft.

Top: A Blackburn Skua naval dive bomber. Above: A section of Blackburn Aircraft floor mosaic dating back to the 1930s, relocated and preserved in the BAE Systems offices. Left: Wartime maintenance on a Gipsy Moth at Brough Flying School.

The approach of the Second World War brought an expansion of production facilities when the Blackburn Shark, a contemporary of the more famous Swordfish, was in production at Brough, along with the Skua naval dive bomber which went on to be the first British aircraft to shoot down an enemy aircraft in the war.

The 1950s saw the introduction of the giant Beverley freighter aircraft and between 1955 and 1958 a total of 47 Beverley aircraft were delivered on schedule to the RAF.

In 1958 the first twin jet, low level, high-speed strike aircraft, the Buccaneer (the first of its kind in the world) made its maiden flight. Over 200 Buccaneers were produced up to 1977 – a 19-year continuous production run.

In the 1960s Blackburn Aircraft was absorbed in to Hawker Siddeley as part of the rationalisation of the UK aerospace industry. It later became British Aerospace in the 1970s and finally BAE Systems at the end of 1999.

Key aircraft produced at Brough have included the Kangaroo, Iris, B2, Shark, Firebrand, Swordfish, Skua, Botha, Barracuda, Beverley, Buccaneer, and of course Hawk with which the site is still heavily involved.

Brough has been associated with the Hawk since the 1970s and indeed has become known as "Home of the Hawk," having been the centre for design and manufacture of the

Above: The prototype of the famous Beverley Aircraft; the Universal Freighter, with the workforce.

worldwide fleet. There are now more than 1,000 Hawks sold or on order around the world.

As part of the Military Air & Information (MAI) business, Brough's primary role is the design, development, manufacture and engineering support of the Hawk advanced jet trainer. The site, covering approximately 17.5 acres of industrial and office space, also houses the company's Structural and Dynamic Test Facility.

The main projects and specialist capabilities cover latest export Hawk aircraft, avionics and mission system development, Hawk airframe manufacture, technical publications and engineering support to the Hawk aircraft fleet. The test facility works on specimens of the company's leading military aircraft including Typhoon and F-35 Lightning II which undergo static, fatigue and environmental testing.

Above: Taking off in the 1920s is the twin engine Blackburn R.T.1 Kangaroo, owned by Blackburn Aircraft subsidiary, North Sea Aerial Navigation Co Ltd, also based at Brough Aerodrome.

The BAE Systems operations which exist on the Brough site owe a lot to the heritage of its predecessors, Blackburn Aircraft, Hawker Siddeley, British Aerospace and its highly-skilled workforce.

As one would expect with such a long history, there have been many changes and the site is more compact than in the past. The aerodrome's airfield, which once operated aircraft from B2 trainers through to the Hawk, is now closed and much of the site has been developed as the Humber Enterprise Park.

What is left is cutting-edge expertise and almost half the manufacturing work which goes in to Hawk, the flying classroom used to train future generations of fast jet pilots for air forces around the world, employing almost 1,000 people at the site.

The sub-assemblies for every aircraft are manufactured in the sheds where Blackburn Aircraft once developed its icons of the past.

Alongside the manufacturing sheds, teams of engineers are also developing the "brains" of the Hawk with facilities once used for heavy manufacturing now home to software development and testing rigs.

Above: Brough workers make their way to the canteen at lunchtime in April 1940. Below: The Blackburn Firebrand MkIV entered service with the Fleet Air Arm just too late to see action in World War Two.

The airborne simulation technology which allows pilots to prepare for life in a front line fighter aircraft is designed, developed and evolved by the engineering teams at Brough.

In a Hawk, a pilot is able to simulate everything from radar and weapons to sensors and defensive aids, allowing them to be "brain

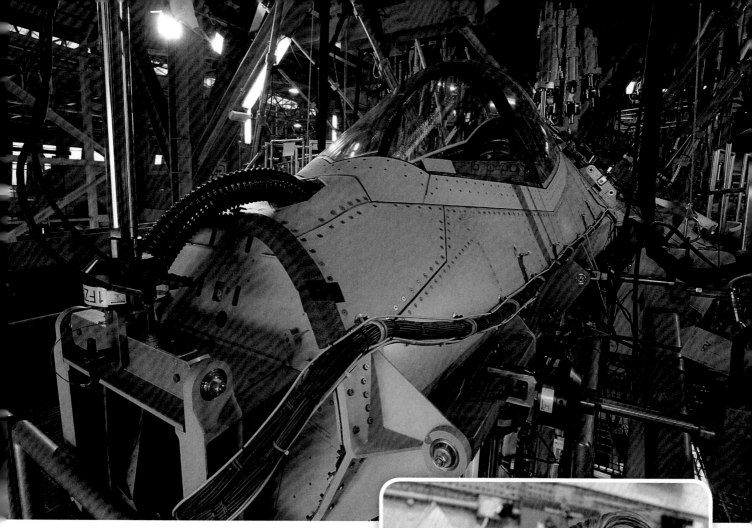

Above: *Third phase of durability testing on an F-35 Lightning II airframe, at Brough.* **Right:** *BAE Systems helps apprentices learn new skills.*

trained" for life flying fast jet aircraft such as the Eurofighter Typhoon or F-35 Lightning II.

The project management team, which supports an international programme serving aircraft flown by 18 nations across the world, is also based at Brough, so it is easy to see why Brough is known as the "Home of the Hawk."

Whilst a UK Hawk sits as a gate guardian at the entrance to the site, it is not the only aircraft that has a presence there.

Above: *BAE Systems is continually investing in facilities at Brough.*

The unique structural and dynamic testing facility at Brough enables BAE Systems to carry out testing work on Eurofighter Typhoon and F-35 Lightning II airframes. The company is a major partner on both programmes.

The test rigs use up to 4,000 strain gauges and more than 150 actuators to push and pull the airframe of the jet to make it think it is "flying."

In February 2016, the site began the third lifetime of structural testing on the F-35 with each lifetime seeing the airframe "flown" for 8,000 hours.

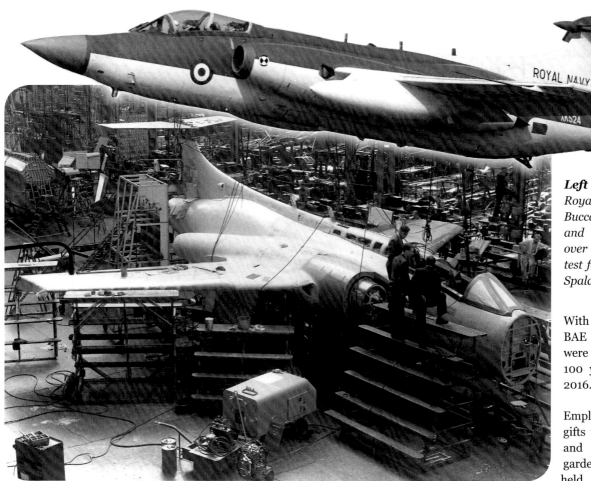

Left and above: A Royal Navy Blackburn Buccaneer in production and taking to the skies over Blackburn flight test facility at Holme-on-Spalding Moor.

With such a proud history BAE Systems and staff were eager to celebrate 100 years of aviation in 2016.

Employees were given gifts throughout the year and a 1940s themed garden party was held on site for employees. A special film was made charting the history and working life on site which was narrated by current and ex-employees and publicity material was produced to mark the occasion.

The structural test team at Brough are experts in their field having rigorously tested a dozen different aircraft types since the 1970s, including Buccaneer, Harrier, Tornado, Hawk and Eurofighter Typhoon.

Above: A Hawk aircraft takes to the skies from Brough.

Above: Hawk Manufacturing at Brough.

The highlight event was the Centenary Day which was a family social occasion for employees and their families. The fun-packed day attracted 5,000 attendees who enjoyed site tours and a programme of entertainment including fairground rides, a circus tent, displays and arena acts, with a flying display in the afternoon.

In addition a group of volunteers built a flying 1/3-scale replica of the first aircraft to fly from Brough – the 1916 GP Seaplane. They also bridged the 100 year technology gap by including a 21st century electronics fit with Data-link, GPS, MEMS Gyroscope, 3D video telemetry etc. The organisers involved over 70 volunteers from 10 local organisations in the project and built the 7.5m wing span seaplane which is now certified for public flying displays by the Civil Aviation Authority.

Students from a local school were also involved in the project in line with the Brough site's comprehensive programme of community investment. This includes charity fundraising and volunteering, early careers liaison with local schools and colleges, sponsorship of events and donations to local organisations, involvement in local community projects and an active Heritage Facility staffed by former employees.

The financial spin-off from this commitment is impressive. Last year more than £56,000 was committed in sponsorship to the local community, and over £9,000 was raised by employees for local charities.

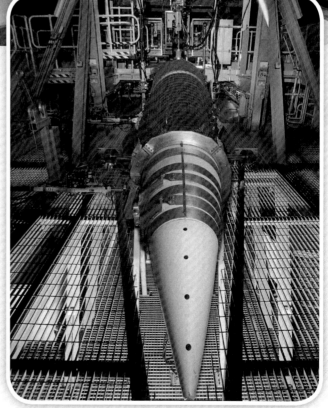

Above: A structural test taking place on a Typhoon.

The Blackburn legacy lives on at Brough, with employees proud to celebrate their 100 year history and community links, and they now look forward to maintaining their reputation for excellence and innovation into the future.

InterTech
25 Years of showcasing their skills

InterTech has a 25 year thoroughbred pedigree in designing world-class showrooms for the automotive industry – the motorcycle industry in particular. Working alongside motorcycle brands like HarleyDavidson, Triumph Motorcycles, Honda, Piaggio and Yamaha, InterTech has created thousands of motorcycle dealer showrooms worldwide. Here, InterTech's main responsibilities are the design, manufacture and provision of the very best quality merchandising fixtures available - from point of sale displays through to sales desks and counters.

The Hull-based company prides itself on being able to supply everything required to create the perfect showroom environment. The process begins with drawings and 3D CGI visualisations to model the showroom interior. This leads on to the selection of showroom lighting, flooring, external signage and interior point of sale graphics. In this way, InterTech really is a one-stop creative shop.

Above: InterTech HQ, Priory Park, Hull. Built in 2010. *Left:* Early days at the drawing board the year 1990.

Services provided to the automotive retail industry range from a total rebranding right through to designing the full interior of a showroom to reflect a client's corporate identity. The company uses carefully selected and approved suppliers to help to deliver a full turnkey solution anywhere in the world. InterTech has provided services and products to over 36 countries with a customer base now spanning 6 continents. Notable milestones include implementing the first Harley-Davidson showroom in Moscow.

The port city of Kingston upon Hull has superb logistics with a vast range of local industrial suppliers and shipping resources. This means that InterTech can now deliver over 150 new showrooms per year – absolutely anywhere.

Above: Piaggio Group store design interior 2013

Above: Honda Showroom by InterTech 2012

In 1986, 21 year-old Andrew Fenton, the son of a Hull trawlerman, began working for a construction company as a joiner and cabinet maker after his apprenticeship. Shortly after that company went into administration, Andrew made the bold decision to set up 'AF Design'; an entirely new kind of design and manufacturing business which later went on to become InterTech.

Andrew explained that before he set up the business he went to Riley High School – a tough, all-boys inner-city school in Hull.

"I just loved woodwork. With the school being a technical school it had all the workshop resources in woodwork, metalwork and plastics. I remember it being a very tough no-nonsense school; frightening at times - but it offered a great grounding in crafts and engineering.

"I remember being amazed at the workshops. I lived in one of the Hull maisonettes in Cavill Place which, though they were brand new at time, had no garage - not even a garden. So when I first saw a proper workshop where you could actually make things – well, that was an epiphany for me.

Above: Sail Training Vessel Malcolm Miller.

"I remember motor science and trying to build a bright orange beach buggy with goal of being able to drive it around the school playing field by the end of term. Then there was the theory of learning all about the combustion engine. Induction, compression, power and exhaust. Or 'suck, squeeze, bang, blow!' – which was the neat phrase that our teacher used to say. Looking back, I think that the woodwork and motor science connection definitely had

Right: Andrew Fenton on the bridge of the Arco Severn, in 1981.

some impact on me, although at the time, I'd no idea just how much.

"Even at my earlier middle school, Villa High in Walker Street, Hull, woodwork had played a key role. Any excuse to get out of rugby practice! I owe a lot to my woodworker teacher Mr. Fox - apart from him giving me very sore sideburns which he would pull if you weren't listening! He helped me a lot; he had a real way of getting you to learn and he laid the foundations of InterTech.

"I left school with no qualifications except a merit badge for woodwork. I remember him saying: 'You may not have any bloody thing down on paper but you have experience - and every time I turn around, you're there - which tells me you're passionate and interested!'

"I was an only child and with my father being at sea all the time, I took Mr. Fox's comments to heart.

"I was brought up on a council estate. I lived in the Troutbeck House block of flats in Cavill Place, off Walker Street, Hull - which was built in the early 70s. This was where the entertainer Joe Longthorne lived for a short time and also where the notorious serial arsonist Peter Dinsdale (alias Bruce Lee) lived. I remember Dinsdale being a bit of a loner and with myself being an only child our paths crossed a number of times over the years. He was a very quiet boy - I had no idea he was to become a serial arsonist or about the people he had been convicted of killing in the various fires he had started. I remember it was a bizarre time. One week, Joe Longthorne would drive down in his Rolls Royce with all the kids running behind the car. My mum would call me in for tea and Joe would be on the TV at the London Palladium! Then there would be the TV news of serial arsonist Peter Dinsdale being convicted. All this happened from the same Hull street! As a young child, nothing seemed unusual. But looking back now, they were crazy times - sometimes sad - but always colourful.

"With the fishing industry in its early decline in the 70s, my dad was spending less time working on fishing trawlers. He was lucky enough to have found work on both the Sail Training Association vessels: the Sir Winston Churchill which was built in 1964 at

Dunston's Ship yard, Hessle - and the Malcolm Miller - the Churchill's sister ship built in 1968, Aberdeen. These ships were training sailing schooners and put a mixture of young kids from different backgrounds together. As a very small child I spent a lot time on both these ships whilst my dad served as the ship's cook.

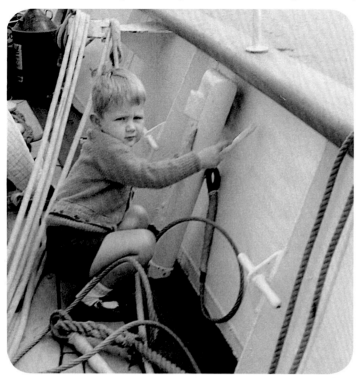

Above: *1969, Andrew aged 3 on the Malcolm Miller.* **Below:** *Seaman Fenton's 'discharge papers' at the age of 12.*

"A lot of my youth was spent on ships. My dad later worked for the dredging company Arco Marine on a number of the company's dredgers, mainly Arco Severn - again serving as cook. I went to sea with my dad from the age of about 8 years of age right up to me leaving school. I took every opportunity that I could to go to

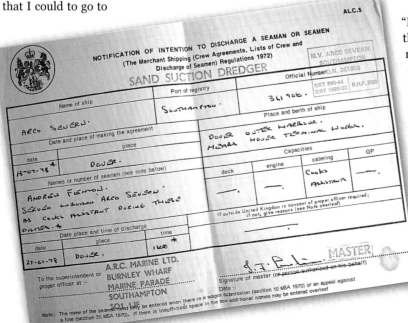

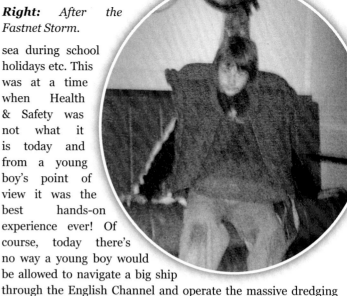

Right: *After the Fastnet Storm.*

sea during school holidays etc. This was at a time when Health & Safety was not what it is today and from a young boy's point of view it was the best hands-on experience ever! Of course, today there's no way a young boy would be allowed to navigate a big ship through the English Channel and operate the massive dredging gear, bringing the suction pipe up from the bottom of the sea bed. There's no way that a mere boy would be allowed to discharge the ship's cargo of aggregate ashore - alone - once the ship had docked. Come to think of it, it probably wasn't really allowed back then...

"I was aged 12 on board the dredger Arco Severn when severe gales hit the famous Cowes Week Regatta in 1979. It was the time of the notorious Fastnet Race which runs from the Isle of Wight to the Fastnet Rock off Ireland and back. During the race an unpredicted and extremely violent storm wreaked havoc on over 300 yachts that were taking part. I remember that Arco Severn was summoned to assist the emergency services and naval forces and help look for survivors. I remember being very frightened on the ship's bridge because the men I was with looked scared and some were seasick. We had gone from calm blue water earlier that day to what I remember as being the impenetrable darkness of a storm that you just could not see.

"But you could certainly hear and feel the movement of the ship struggling to right itself. Every time the ship rolled you could hear the roar of the boiling sea getting closer. Then the ship would lurch the opposite way. I remember the mate telling me to keep a sharp lookout for flares and wreckage and to keep watch - which we all did, all night. That storm took 18 lives; 3 of them being rescuers. One thing that stuck in my memory was that so many of the crew slept through the storm on our ship. I was told not to wake any of them under any circumstances. Not understanding why at the time, I got very angry that they were allowed to sleep. I remember the ship's Master telling me that we had all the men needed to deal with the issue and that if the storm lasted any longer then the tired crew would need relieving. I was truly put in my place! It's under these type of circumstance that you really do grow up, very fast. That experience as a young boy for me was something I will never forget.

"Aged 13 I sat the exam for the Trinity House School in Hull. As luck would have it – I failed to get in, so my career at sea was not be. I loved going to sea with my dad and I carried doing that right up to leaving school.

"My mum was manageress of the Beautyfarm cosmetics shop on Hessle Road in Hull. The shop was owned by local pharmacy chain Foster and Plumpton. From the age of 16 I worked as a Saturday boy in the shop and I helped out with maintenance on the building. My mother was very retail minded and was always looking for innovative ways of pulling customers into the shop. So I was given the job of building all the displays. Though I didn't realise it at the time, that was the start of my understandings of a retail environment and how it worked and functioned for both the customers and the shop staff.

"The company had its own joinery workshop that looked after the 20 or so shops they owned and so I was offered a job as an apprentice joiner, kick-starting my joinery career. I worked with my boss Doug Pepper who taught me the skills needed to become a good joiner. I later went to the Hull College for 5 years and gained an apprenticeship as a joiner and woodwork machinist.

"After finishing my apprenticeship in 1987 I began work at a new shop-fitting company for about 3 to 4 years. I started as a joiner then progressed to a setter-outer - producing drawings for furniture – on a real drawing board! I remember it gave me a good understanding how to build things. I worked on various projects including local shopping centres, roll out like Littlewood catalogue shops to bespoke projects like Filofax showroom in London.

"Sadly, the company went into administration. The 1980s was a boom and bust time with a lot of uncertainty. However, after an unsatisfactory period working for a number of other joinery

Above: Fitting at the Filofax London Boutique 1988. **Below:** One of the latest Triumph Motorcycle Showrooms completed in 2017.

companies, I decided to start my own business as a joiner. I was 23 at the time. That business was called 'AF Design' and over the first few years I worked as a sole-trader from my van with no premises.

"Through local supplier Eyeline Visual Merchandising based on Sutton Fields in Hull, I was able to rent some office space and a limited amount of factory space. This helped me to start a small joinery division and we started to make furniture for general shop-fitting projects. I produced a lot of fixtures and cabinets for local coach building company GP Massey in Market Weighton. They also produced a lot of specialised vehicles for various F1 racing teams and also manufactured custom vehicle trailers for the MOD. I supplied some very bespoke furniture for these projects. One project was making hardwood cabinets from iroko which were used by the military to store batteries for the Harrier Jump Jet. In another project we had to build a transportable meeting table strong enough to accommodate an F1 racing car on top of it. The work was somewhat challenging at the time but great to be involved with.

Above: *The temporary location of the 'Last Trip' Memorial to Lost Fishermen at InterTech's head office December 20th,2015 which was the first unveiling of the memorial. The following year is was relocated to Trinity House former school grounds.*

The Last Trip Memorial

Thanks to the Trustees of Trinity House for making this possible. This location is in a setting surrounded by hundreds of years of maritime history and will be a fitting location for this memorial to all the men lost at sea.

Can we also thank the Hull Bullnose Heritage Group and Hull City Council for their support and help with making this possible. And a very big thank you goes to all the families who's loved ones did not return.

To find out more about the Last Trip Memorial please visit www.thelasttrip. co.uk

Right: *An engraved commemorative ship's bow in polished stainless steel.*

"1992 was the point at which I was introduced to Harley-Davidson Motorcycles, who had a mutual contact with Eyeline. Together, we starting to look at building a range of new dealer showrooms that they had planned for expanding their UK dealer network. And this was when I first became involved in designing motorcycle showrooms. I ended up designing stores for locations throughout the UK and Europe. This was my first experience of doing business overseas and it was a great success. It was at the introduction of the European single currency which help make things a lot easier when it came to financing. Because of that, we started to do even more business overseas.

"I remember that hardly anybody had email at that time. With Harley-Davidson being based in the United States, I was one of the few early adopters of email - which I thought was amazing. I was all set up on an IBM machine - the only problem was that I had only one email contact!

"In 2003, after 14 years of working on many motorcycle showrooms for Harley-Davidson, we were approached by Triumph Motorcycles to get involved in a new corporate identity that they were trying to implement within their existing global dealer network. Before that, I had only ever been involved in implementing stores in mainland Europe, so the request for working on their requirements globally was rather daunting. In the first year alone, I remember carrying out dealer surveys in well over 20 countries and taking over 300 international flights. And up to now, InterTech has completed 645 showrooms around the world; many of the components being manufactured in Hull.

"Since then, we have offered our design and manufacturing services for many mainstream brands, for example: Honda, Piaggio Group and Yamaha. We've worked on various bespoke design projects in many different countries creating interior designs for retail, healthcare, visitor centres, bars and restaurants.

"We have also used our knowledge and skills for a number of local community projects. In 2016 we designed 'The Last Trip' – an interactive memorial to the lost fishermen of Hull. The city lost many thousands of men to that unforgiving industry. With my father's side of the family all going to sea it has always been something in which I've taken a personal interest.

"When we designed the Last Trip memorial, I was keen to make people aware of the impact that the fishing Industry had on places

Above: Swiss Hutless Karts and Showroom, Lyss, Switzerland in 2000. *Below:* Andrew Managing Director of InterTech: I am proud to be the son of a Hull fisherman: proud to have grown up and built a business in the city that used to stink of fish when I was a lad. Great times.

like Hull. And with Hull and Grimsby once being the world's largest fishing ports, I wanted to design a memorial that would reflect the sacrifices which these men made - both in peace time and during the defence of this country. Up to now, there has been very little commemoration of those seafaring men considering what they went through and what they achieved."

Smith & Nephew
Hull roots spread worldwide

One of the city's most successful companies has grown from a small pharmacy shop into a global medical technology business employing around 1,000 people locally and over 15,000 across the world.

It was way back in 1856 when Smith & Nephew was founded by Thomas James Smith at Whitefriargate in what was then the heart of the shopping and commercial community. He trained as a pharmacist and was a member of the Royal Pharmaceutical Society.

At that time doctors' visits were expensive and pharmacists were often the first ones consulted. Most medicines did not require a prescription, and factory-made pills were only beginning to displace concoctions produced by doctors and pharmacists.

TJ Smith also took advantage of his close proximity to the docks and the fishermen of Hull and became involved in the wholesale trade of bandages and related materials. He soon built himself an excellent reputation but his main product at the time was cod liver oil.

Above: Thomas James Smith, the man who started Smith & Nephew.

Today, it's difficult to understand how important and valued cod liver oil was in the 19th century.

It was deemed precious oil and its positive effects had long been recorded by doctors.

By the mid-1800s cod liver oil was widely used in hospitals to treat tuberculosis, rickets, malnutrition, osteomalacia (softening of the bones) and some eye conditions. Its popularity continued to grow into the 20th century and cod liver oil is still part of a healthy diet for millions of people today due to its essential vitamins, especially D and A.

TJ Smith was well aware of its popularity and he made numerous trips to Norway in his quest to refine his own cod liver oil for which there was no shortage of customers. Not only was it widely used in hospitals, it was also common practice for family members to all have a spoonful of cod liver oil daily. The product became the springboard from which the business diversified and thrived.

In 1860 TJ Smith took over the lease of 10, North Church Side, alongside Holy Trinity Church in the Old Town, paying a rent of

Above: Early beginnings at North Church Side.

£18 per year. He promoted himself as a "Wholesale Druggist and Cod Liver Oil Merchant" with the majority of his turnover due to trade with hospitals.

With business going well he acquired the property next door and converted it into a small factory.

A commitment to good quality products successfully boosted the reputation of TJ Smith and he built up a large customer base of hospitals. Hull General Infirmary, York and Lincoln County Hospitals were joined by Great Ormond Street, King's College and St Thomas's among others.

TJ Smith's frequent trips to Norway to ensure his cod liver oil was of the highest quality had long been recognised, and in 1883 he received an official accolade when it was awarded a gold medal for quality at an international fisheries exhibition in London.

The business continued to expand, but TJ Smith then fell ill in 1895. He had no son to take over the business so his nephew, Horatio Nelson Smith, joined the business. It is at that time it first became known as Smith & Nephew.

It was to prove a baptism of fire for young HN Smith because just three months later TJ Smith passed away and he was left in charge of the business as just 22 years of age. Fortunately, HN Smith proved himself to be a natural entrepreneur.

Like his uncle, he was a pioneer and was keen to provide new products for customers and had a flair for marketing and selling.

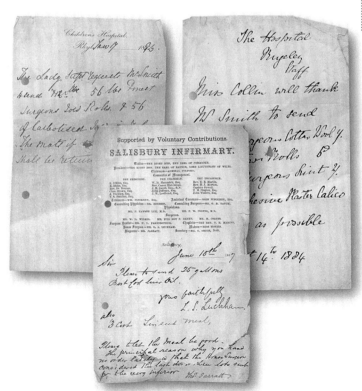

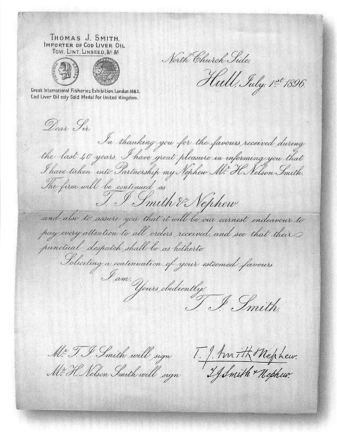

Above: Some of the first orders sent to Thomas James Smith.
Right: The Notice of Partnership signed by Thomas James Smith and his nephew Horatio Nelson Smith.

Soon, HN Smith decided to move away from cod liver oil to capitalise on the growing healthcare market concentrating on wound care products.

Steady expansion continued as new business was successfully sought. HN Smith himself made frequent trips abroad to attract many more hospitals to the customer base of Smith & Nephew.

New premises were needed to meet the demands of business and 5, Neptune Street, still part of the present site in Hull at the top of Hessle Road, were bought for £2,000.

Rapid expansion was just around the corner as the horrors of warfare in the 20th century meant there would be a nearly insatiable demand for wound care products.

Shortly after World War 1 was declared in September 1914, HN Smith was meeting with the envoy of the French President in London. The result was a massive contract for £350,000 for surgical and field dressings.

Such a contract, a huge sum at the time and which would have been worth several millions today, transformed the business and brought the obvious operational problems for HN Smith and his team.

Above: A passport belonging to Horatio Nelson Smith and a first world war field dressing package.
Below: During the war years women boosted production.

To meet the demands of World War 1 Smith & Nephew had to expand at an unprecedented pace with staff numbers rising from 50 to a mind-boggling 1,200. Throughout the war HN Smith was travelling extensively in Europe picking up orders and the company sold dressings to both the UK Government and its allies.

Above: A site built at Clayton, Victoria, Australia during the expansion boom in the 1950s.

When the war ended in 1918 the subsequent lull in orders for wound care products followed and staff numbers reduced to around 200, but HN Smith was determined to find new products in the continually expanding healthcare market. A significant new product which became a feature in most homes in the developed world was Elastoplast.

It was HN Smith's friend, Johannes Lohmann who had invented an elasticated cloth, spread with adhesive in 1924. Seeing the huge potential of this product HN Smith was keen to get involved and in 1930 Smith & Nephew were assigned the rights. The company's Neptune Street site was expanded and by 1937 Smith & Nephew was listed on the London Stock Exchange.

The business continued to be a major supplier of army surgical field dressings and with the outbreak of World War II in 1939 orders again rocketed.

Like many businesses, Smith & Nephew, had to cope with many of its male workers being called up for military service. But, the women of Hull came to the rescue and accounted for 90 per cent of the workforce during those difficult years. World War II also brought with it the real prospect of the company premises being bombed but that didn't deter the workforce who met the challenges set for them.

Finally, when war ended in 1945 Smith & Nephew began re-establishing overseas trade and had ambitious expansion plans. Another key product in the company portfolio at that time was a plaster of Paris bandage known as Gypsona. That product, along with Elastoplast, offered most potential and became the most important marketing tools. Growth also came through acquisition as Smith & Nephew bought Herts Pharmaceuticals and through that acquired the Nivea range.

The popularity of Elastoplast brought about an unusual link with Mount Everest ahead of the first ever ascent in 1953. The climbers' asked Smith & Nephew to develop a special version of Elastoplast

Left: How an Elastoplast product used to look. *Below:* An early example of the plaster of Paris bandage known as Gypsona.

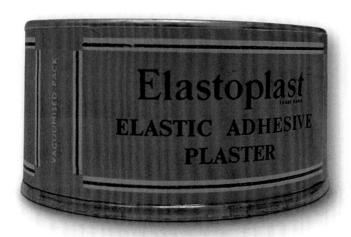

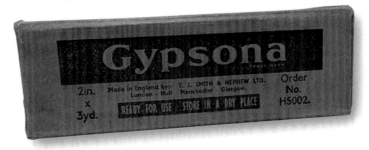

which would still adhere at the very low temperatures they would experience on the climb. This was done and included in the medical supplies. Fortunately, the special Elastoplast wasn't needed for the original intention, but was instead used to seal cylinders of camera film – and that ensured the world got to see photographs from the historic ascent.

As Smith & Nephew progressed through the 1950s and 1960s several new sites were opened overseas in the United States, Canada, Australia, New Zealand and South Africa. The company's research and development team was also busy creating new opportunities around plastics, orthopaedics and wound healing.

The 1980s and early 1990s marked a period of major acquisition for Smith & Nephew which established the company as a world leader in orthopaedics and endoscopy equipment. It was in 1986 that Richards Medical Company was acquired. This was a specialist in orthopaedic products and was bought for £192.7 million which was the largest acquisition up to that date. The U.S. company was based in Memphis, Tennessee.

Another U.S. company was bought in 1988 which complemented the newly acquired Richards range. This was Dyonics which was well placed in the specialised cameras and video sector of arthroscopy. Smith & Nephew still have a site at that base in Andover, Massachusetts. In 1995, another U.S. based business, Acufex Miscrosurgical Inc, followed which promoted Smith & Nephew into a market leader in arthroscopic surgical devices.

The business ethos of expansion and pioneering product development has kept Smith & Nephew ahead of its competitors and in recent years it has capitalised on new opportunities from the emerging markets such as China, Brazil, Saudi Arabia, United Arab Emirates, India, Russia and Costa Rica. In fact, Smith & Nephew now has a presence in more than 100 countries.

It's all a long way from those early days in Hull at Whitefriargate, but the company has never forgotten its roots. In 2011 Smith & Nephew invested approximately £50 million in capital projects at the Hull site. This included bringing the manufacturing of their complex silver coating technology for ACTICOAT silver dressings to Hull and installing a film extrusion manufacturing line. The core technology for this manufacturing process was itself developed in Hull and is a bespoke piece of equipment, specially made for the manufacture of their unique film for a range of wound dressings, including ALLEVYN foam dressings and IV3000 IV site film dressings.

Top and right: *Dyonics and Acufex products which are now under the Smith & Nephew umbrella.*

Not long after this major investment, unfortune struck in 2013 when the Hull facility was badly impacted by the highly unusual levels of flooding which hit the region. Damage was caused across the entire ground floor including the manufacturing and office areas. Through great teamwork the recovery was swift and manufacturing was soon re-started to minimise disruption to customers. Since then, Smith & Nephew have spent £3 million on new flood defences to help protect the site against any repeat events.

Hull remains a high-tech centre for the company and is home to the most high-technology wound care products on the market. Over the past few years new pioneering products have been introduced such as the PICO negative pressure system, DURAFIBER gelling fibre dressings and ALLEVYN Life foam dressings which are all made in the city.

Going forward future plans for the Hull site include a continued focus on the development and launch of new products and it will be the home of complex manufacturing processes.

Smith & Nephew has provided employment for thousands of Hull families for the last 160 years and it has also been actively supporting local good causes alongside the community which founded this global company. Charities supported include the Hull People's Memorial, Whizz Kids and Emmaus. Other links include sponsorship of the Humberside Police's "Lifestyle" Initiative, support for the nearby Adelaide Primary School and the Ron Dearing University Technical College.

Smith & Nephew is also proud be a Major Partner of Hull 2017 UK City of Culture.

Support for healthcare professionals is given in more than 100 countries to help them improve the lives of their patients. This is done by taking a pioneering approach to the design of their advanced medical products and services, and securing wider access to their diverse technologies for more customers globally.

The latest results show annual sales were more than £3.2 billion – a figure which would have been unimaginable in the early days for TJ Smith. His nephew, HN Smith passed away in 1960 after a lifetime driving the business forward, and he would have been proud that one of the great successes from Hull's industrial past is still flourishing today at home and abroad.

Right: MP Alan Johnson opens the new £3 million flood defences in Hull. *Below:* Hull and Proud: Smith & Nephew are a Major Partner of Hull 2017 City of Culture.

Above: Spencer Group cable crawler, developed for access to suspension bridge cable spans and dehumidification.

Spencer Group British Engineering
A home-grown success story

Spencer Group, established in 1989 specialise in large engineering projects ranging from the design and build of green power stations, working across the UK rail network and building and maintaining complex suspension bridges. The company has an entrepreneurial spirit and a long history of delivering innovation in a variety of other sectors utilising its civil engineering expertise.

The business was founded by Executive Chairman, Charlie Spencer OBE from his home in Anlaby with just two employees. Today, Spencer Group employs over 400 people and has offices in London and Glasgow but its headquarters remain in Hull, East Yorkshire.

*Left: Company founder Charlie Spencer. **Above:** Charlies house in Anlaby, where he started the business in 1989. **Right:** Charlies first two employees Dave Evans and Harry Lindley.*

Spencer Group has found success by adopting an approach to 'self-deliver' all aspects of the engineering process from design through to delivery. This has proven highly successful on logistically challenging engineering projects, such as the £200m project 'Energy Works', an environment-friendly power plant on a 12-acre site on the east bank of the River Hull. It will be the first facility of its kind in the UK, using a combination of innovative renewable energy technologies that produce the most favourable results in terms of recycling and air quality.

*Above: A 3D rendering for Energy Works, the £200 million environmentally-friendly power plant in Hull. **Below:** Charlie (far left) on site.*

The project is the largest privately funded power station of its type and will produce enough electricity to power the equivalent of 43,000 homes, by processing 240,000 tonnes of waste a year. Energy Works, which goes live in 2018, will deliver a renewable energy plant to Hull and to provide job opportunities to people in the city. The project has been awarded a grant of almost £20 million from the European Regional Development Fund (ERDF) in recognition of the role it can play in encouraging further innovation in this field. In addition, private investors from around the world have funded the project leading to a £200m scheme.

The business also works extensively in the rail sector, designing and building rail stations and depot's, this is particularly pertinent given the UK's investment into Rail electrification. The company is currently working on a highly complex tunnelling project at Finsbury Park station in central London, designing and delivering two 15metre deep shafts between Victoria and Piccadilly in the London Underground network.

Locally the company has delivered a number of projects, including remodelling Hull's Paragon Station; Victoria Dock Lock; Millennium Bridge - The Deep; East Park Restoration; Dehumidification on the main cables of the Humber Bridge.

The Humber Bridge project involved the use of a unique "Cable Crawler" gantry system which was first designed and developed by Spencer Group in 2007 which has propelled the company to be a world leader in high-level bridge works. Spencer Group has then gone on to use the system to enable vital dehumidification work to prevent corrosion of cables on the Severn, Forth Road and Humber suspension bridges, as well as the Alvsborg Bridge in Sweden and the Great Belt Bridge in Denmark – the world's largest retro-fit cable dehumidification project.

141

The business has designed and built several landmark structures across the UK and achieved several 'firsts' in the industry, key dates throughout the Spencer Group history include:

1989 - Established Spencer Group.

1989 - Company starts out undertaking marine piling and specialist civil works.

1992 - Order book extended to include first Rail-related projects, including work on railway stations, bridges, depots and terminals.

1998 - Scottish Bridge of Invention at Irvine – the first retracting footbridge in the UK.

1999 - Won entry onto their first procurement framework with Network Rail as a design and delivery partner for the Station Delivery Partnership. The company also established its relationship with Stagecoach as preferred contractor following completion of its fifth bus depot.

2001 - Fraserburgh Ship Lift – the first commercial ship lift in the UK.

2006 - Increased development of its in-house multi-disciplinary capabilities, exemplified by the award of a series of contracts to design and deliver signalling control centres for Network Rail. A project was awarded to Spencer Group to refurbish and remodel Paragon Station in Hull.

2007 - Spencer Group developed a unique process to enable work at high level to "de-humidify" cables on suspension bridges and

Above: One of Charlies first projects, the Tidal Barrier, Hull.

applied this first on the Forth Road Bridge in Scotland. In 2010 similar work was carried out to protect cables on the Humber Bridge from corrosion.

2010 - Delivered first biomass handling projects including the UK's first biomass import terminal for the Port of Tyne and Drax Power Ltd.

2011 - Acquired the former ADM Cocoa Mills site at Cleveland Street to develop Energy Works project.

2012 - Bought and moved into new headquarters at the One Humber Quays office overlooking the Humber on Hull Marina, and for the first time one of Yorkshire's most prestigious office buildings was fully occupied.

2013 - First contract with Transport for London at New Cross Gate Depot.

2013 - World's largest retro-fitted bridge dehumidification project began on Great Belt Bridge, Denmark.

2014 - Company hits £100m turnover for the first time.

2016 - Energy Works construction starts, first facility of its kind in the UK.

2017 & beyond - The company is ideally situated to continue its progression in its core markets with a strong pipeline of work identified.

Spencer Group is very passionate about people and has a deep commitment to developing young talent. The company has invested heavily in apprentices in the last three years taking on 24 local young people in IT, Construction, Business Administration, Design and Resources, of these 15 have permanent roles within the business and the rest are progressing well.

The company is also a principle sponsor of the Ron Dearing University Technical College (UTC) in Hull, which aims to enable local young people to thrive in the digital economy and provide employers with the advanced technical skills they require. Spencer Group is making major, practical commitments to the UTC, including significant input into curriculum development; providing one-to-one mentors; setting business projects for students; providing high-quality work placements; and guaranteeing job interviews at the end of their course.

In 2013 the company became the first engineering business in the UK, and the first private sector

Right and below: *Hull Paragon Station has received many thousands of visitors - including HM The Queen.*

business in East Yorkshire, to become an accredited Living Wage employer. An active advocate of ethical pay, conducting a series of interviews with local, regional and national media to promote the Living Wage campaign. Other initiatives include supporting the Armed Forces Corporate Covenant as an armed forces-friendly organisation. The commitments of the covenant include actively

Above: Millennium Bridge, The Deep, Hull.

seeking to support the employment of ex-servicemen and women and their spouses or partners.

Spencer Groups awards over the years have included being named Humber Renewables Large Business of the Year in the Humber Renewables Awards; winner of the Transport Supplier of the Year at the National Transport Awards; winner of the Best Large Project on Britain's railways in the Network Rail Partnership Awards for work on a major rail improvement scheme in Ipswich; winner of the Collaborative Working Award (with Medway Council, Atkins and Balfour Beatty) in the Network Rail Partnership Awards for East Kent re-signalling project; winner of the Rail Infrastructure/Possessions Team of the Year in the Rail Staff Awards for the Gravesend Station re-modelling project; and winner of the Best Large Project of the Year in the Railway Industry Innovation Awards for the Gravesend scheme.

Charlie Spencer himself has been honoured. He was awarded an OBE for services to business and the economy in 2015 and presented with the Lifetime Contribution Award at the 2016

Above: Dehumidification on the Humber Bridge.

Above and inset: *Spencer Group headquarters at the city's impressive One Humber Quays overlooking the Humber on Hull Marina.*

Hull Daily Mail Business Award for his contribution to the business community in his home city.

Charlie said;

"The success of Spencer Group is testament to the great people employed by the business and I am very proud of all our employees and their achievements over the last 28 years"

"Our values have been with the company since 1989 and continue to guide Spencer Group's ambitious plans for further growth and the company's quest to be recognised as a flagship for the very best of British engineering".

Right: *Charlie Spencer receives the Hull Daily Mail Business Award for his contribution to the business community in his home city.*

Arco
Experts in Safety

With its Head Office in Waverley Street, Hull, and more than 50 locations throughout the UK as well as offices in Ireland and China, Arco Limited is the UK's leading supplier of personal protective equipment, workwear and workplace safety products.

The Hull-based, fourth generation family owned business with a heritage spanning over 132 years now has over 60,000 customers and an annual turnover approaching £300m. Through its product catalogue and a strong nationwide sales office network, Arco is an expert in safety, offering a world class range of 170,000 quality assured, branded and own-brand products, carefully selected from ethically compliant suppliers. Products include personal protective equipment, clothing, footwear, gloves, workplace safety and hygiene products, as well as safety training and consultancy services. Arco is one of Hull's largest employers with over 850 people employed in its Waverley Street Head Office and National Distribution Centre.

The firm was established in 1884 to supply a range of rubber products to industry and the Martin family joined the business soon thereafter. Some manufacturing was also undertaken, said

Above: An early 20th century picture of Arco's shop in Hull.
Below: Arco's National Distribution Centre, Hull.

to have included the production of tennis balls for the then little-known championship at Wimbledon!

The company moved from London to Hull in 1890 and Thomas Martin became Managing Director in 1907 after a distinguished career in the Navy. His son, the second Thomas Martin, succeeded him. The company survived a World War 2 bombing raid that destroyed its King Edward Street premises in May 1941, including all of its sales records. This could have signalled the end, but not one customer failed to settle all accounts due.

In 1959 the third generation Tom Martin joined the business, followed by his brother Stephen in 1964, and on becoming Joint Managing Directors in 1968 embarked on a vigorous programme of expansion, establishing branches throughout the country. The firm's 49th retail store was opened in Cambridge in 2016.

In 1961, the company moved to purpose built premises on its present site in Waverley Street, and in 2000 a new state of the art National Distribution Centre was opened on Henry Boot Way. This purpose built 200,000 square foot facility is externally supported, creating totally clear space inside, and the building won awards for its innovative design.

In 1988 Tom Martin's son, Thomas, joined the business, followed by Stephen's daughter, Jo, in 2000. In 2002, Thomas and Jo became Joint Managing Directors, with Stephen Martin appointed Vice Chairman.

Under their leadership Arco made significant changes to its supply chain management and established the Arco Clothing Centre in Preston. That same year, Nicholas Hildyard joined Arco as Finance Director following a career at Smith and Nephew. Tom Martin retired from the business in 2006, being appointed as Life President, and remains a Non Executive Director along with brother, Stephen.

Nicholas Hildyard was appointed Joint Managing Director with Thomas Martin in 2008 following the sad death of Jo Martin at the age of just 39. Upon Nick's retirement in 2012, Neil Jowsey, formerly Arco Sales & Marketing Director, joined Thomas in leading the company.

In July 2014, Richard Martin, son of Stephen Martin, re-joined Arco, having enjoyed seven years of flying, as an opportunity came up at Arco to lead their transformational change projects. Richard took the role of IT and Change Director. In 2017, Richard is spearheading the company's digital transformation strategy as Digital Director.

Over the course of more than a century, Arco has grown from a small jobbing merchant to the country's leading supplier of personal protective equipment, workwear

147

Above: The Arco retail store, Ashton. *Below:* Newly installed mezzanine level and packing benches at the National Distribution Centre.

and workplace safety products. Tom Martin attributes Arco's success to "determination and the ability to adapt to changing circumstances...we are now carrying the best of our traditional values forward in the 21st century."

Arco works with strategic suppliers to offer premium industry brands and also invests expertise in the design and development of innovative new products under own brands Arco, Arco Essentials, Trojan, Buffalo and Arco Pro. Arco works with its customers to understand their needs and provide solutions that have been designed by experts, tested to the right standards and are fit for the job. As a family owned business, Arco is driven by the needs of its customers rather than shareholder value, and has an established record as a profitable company making a positive contribution to the industry and helping to shape the safety world.

In 2016, Arco completed significant enhancements to its National Distribution Centre (NDC), creating additional capacity and improving service and delivery capabilities. The £4 million investment forms part of the company's expansion plans and includes the construction of a new mezzanine floor, doubling the number of pack benches. The investment also included additional software upgrades and conveyor systems, all of which increase the company's picking and packing capability for orders and enhance the ability to meet increasing customer delivery demands.

This investment is just the start of more exciting plans for Arco, as the business unveils further news for growth. In 2016, the company submitted plans to build a brand new distribution centre (NDC2) on the land adjacent to the company's existing distribution centre, which could create over 200 potential new jobs in the local area. The proposed 220,000 square foot building will house both additional warehouse and logistics capabilities and will enable the organisation to double its output, providing supply chain

infrastructure to support new developments in 2017.

Arco is dedicated to its Corporate Social Responsibility (CSR) and supports a number of organisations and projects as part of its commitment. Each year the company donates more than 1% of profit to charities. Arco's community programme has three main objectives:

- To give something back to local communities.

- To support its people in the things that matter to them.

- To uphold Arco core values - Respect for People, Excellence in Reputation and Hard Work and Enterprise.

To ensure these objectives are achieved, community activity is organised into three focus areas: Community Volunteering; Charitable Fundraising and Partnerships.

Above: The Yorkshire Air Ambulance.

Arco continues to work on its ethical strategy, which first started over a decade ago, and was pleased to see amendments to company disclosure requirements under the Modern Slavery Act 2015. This motivated the company to launch its own 'Start Yours' campaign, which involved Arco making a number of recommendations to businesses who buy safety equipment to raise awareness and guide businesses to ensure ethical compliance.

Arco's core values are deeply embedded in the company's purpose – keeping people safe at work. Putting customers and people at the centre of everything it does is something the company firmly believes in and has made Arco the company that it is today.

Above: Teams competing in our Arco Family Fun Day dragon boat race. *Right:* Designers of the Hull City of Culture Volunteers' uniforms with Rosie Millard, Chair of Hull UK City of Culture 2017.

Arco is proud to be a major partner and the official volunteer uniform supplier for the Hull UK City of Culture 2017. As part of its commitment to the initiative, the company designed and sourced the official uniform to be worn by over 4,000 volunteers. Other projects include long term support for the Yorkshire Air Ambulance, the Lifestyle Project and Macmillan Cancer Support.

Arco takes its ethical responsibility seriously and was the first distributor within the industry to become a member of the Ethical Trading Initiative (ETI). Arco joined the ETI in 2007, forming part of an alliance of leading companies, trade unions and voluntary organisations that work in partnership to improve the lives of workers around the globe.

Dunston Ship Repairs
A proud heritage and exciting future

Shipbuilding has come a long way in the last 150 years since Richard Dunston started out building wooden barges miles from the sea.

Today, Dunston Ship Repairs Ltd, now based at William Wright Dock, in Hull, offers a wide range of maritime services to keep modern-day vessels in tip-top condition.

Before the company was formed in 1858 Richard Dunston owned a boatyard at Torksey on the Foss Dyke, Lincolnshire. He sold that to establish another at Thorne on the Stainforth and Keadby Canal – 12 miles from the River Trent and 45 miles from the sea.

The wooden barges he built were made from hand-sawn timber grown locally. It was a self-contained boatyard and he was able to make sails, ropes and running gear. Ropes, in particular were very popular at that time and proved a lucrative side line as they were used in many different businesses, and the shipyard ropery supplied coir, hemp, manilla and cotton ropes.

Below: The Rix Cheetah which was converted to a much larger vessel at Dunston (Ship Repairs) in 2016.

Above: The Ocean Reliance which Dunston (Ship Repairs) converted from a roll-on roll-off ferry to a state-of-the art survey vessel returned to William Wright Dock for its 5 year Special Survey.

The ships' chandlers in Hull and Grimsby also used the shipyard for the supply of ships' blocks, masts, spars, boat hooks, boat oars, sails and covers.

Above: The Sandsend Dredger on which the digger was fitted at the Dunston premises.

Repairs to old wooden hulls formed most of the early work but gradually vessels capable of carrying 80 tonnes were built and were used on the Humber and the surrounding tributaries.

Ships were mostly clinker built and it was only in the later years of wooden shipbuilding that the carvel form of construction became popular. In carvel construction a smooth hull is created that is stronger than a clinker built hull.

Richard Dunston died in 1902 and in subsequent years new generations of the family have run the business.

With rapid changes in the early 20th century the life of the wooden barge was nearing its end. New buildings and plant were being used for the construction of iron and steel ships and with every passing year bigger and wider vessels were in demand.

A problem then arose because while the crafts could be built in the shipyard, they could not pass through the canal to the sea. So, in 1932, Dunston's bought the shipyard of Henry Scarr Ltd, on Hessle-on-Humber to overcome that problem.

Right: A new crane which was fitted to the Cherry Sand.

Various vessels were constructed and additional works including the joinery and fittings, installation of the main and auxiliary machinery, and electrical equipment were all completed in-house.

The Second World War years brought a boom for the company which became a pioneer in the use of electric welding. In 1942 it was decided to set aside part of the shipyard for the construction of all-welded ships, which at that time were still unusual.

Soon, Dunston's became leaders in this field as it was able to develop the best bulk production of all-welded ships of the smaller type. The Admiralty came calling for which 159 all-welded tugs of one type were produced.

With the smooth workflow that had been developed, the completed ships were leaving the shipyard at six-day intervals. Many other crafts were also built during the war for the Admiralty and afterwards for foreign governments.

The first all-welded trawler to be built in this country came from the yard, and the great majority of tugs ordered for the Thames since 1936 have come from either the Thorne or Hessle yards.

From the 1940s to 1960s barges and lighter tugs were mainly produced and later coastal tankers.

In 1974 the Dunston family sold the Hessle and Thorne yards to the Ingram Corporation of America and the yards remained American owned until 1985 when they were put up for sale again. The Thorne yard was closed and the Hessle yard was part of a management buy-out.

From the 1980s production included Clyde car ferries, a cargo ship, gas tankers and naval tugs.

Right: Other dry dockings at William Wright Dock have included the Alba Na Mara, (Top) Putford Aires, (right) and the Hirta (top, opposite).

The mid-1990s saw the company concentrate solely on the ship repair business as it modified its core business to suit the needs of the commercial market.

Richard Dunston built his business on a proud tradition of innovation, quality and reliability which was recognised throughout the maritime industry. That approach remains a mainstay of the business today which moves with the times to ensure best standards in all areas of operations.

Innovative working practices that produce quality results and ensure the completion of projects on time are introduced continually.

Whilst the last few decades has seen a concentration on ship repair and restoration work, there is now a growing demand within the offshore energy sector, and consequently, Dunston is working to establish its name within the ship building sector once more.

It is currently utilising its strong reputation to demonstrate confidence with its current client base, and hopes to build new relationships throughout the industry and establish the company's products as a market leader within that sector.

Facilities surrounding the dry dock including machinery workshop, plumbers' workshop, engine cleaning bay, shipwright and joinery workshop, fabrication and welding hall, sheet metal workshop, carnage facilities, specialised equipment and machinery including laser alignment local specialist marine services and materials.

Workshops are fully equipped with an impressive array of specialised machinery to support engineers, fabricators, plumbers, electricians, joiners and shipwrights.

The aim of the company remains, as it always has been, in that it strives to meet customers' expectations on every occasion whatever their needs. Throughout the range of services supplied, the business works hard to utilise the advances in technology to develop more innovative approaches and ensure best working practices are in place.

That can't be done without a valued and highly skilled workforce and Dunston's is keen to promote ongoing staff development. Its employment packages include training and development opportunities at all levels and that investment in personnel is a demonstration of the company's commitment to providing the results its customers expect.

Staff have the benefit of working only with the industry leading specialist equipment and only the best materials are used on company projects.

Dunston's is also keen to support its roots and where possible it sources products locally and consideration for the environment is built into all of its procurement processes.

Customers are kept informed of progress at all times from negotiation through to completion to ensure excellent communication channels at all levels. On completion of projects feedback is sought to ensure that best practice methods continue to be fostered into services.

Today, there are two principal companies within the Dunston organisation: Dunston Ship Repairs and Dunston Electrical. Each of these companies offers a wide range of maritime services providing quality as a benchmark and a willingness to arrange work patterns around the needs of customers' schedules and deadlines.

Around 75-80 people are employed by Dunston's and between 25 to 30 vessels dock annually. Repairs are also carried out to vessels

Right: Installation of new machinery.

which do not require dry docking. Further work is also generated in the local community with the company policy of using local suppliers and sub-contractors wherever possible.

Although Dunston was accredited to ISO 9001:2008 the business has now successfully been accredited to ISO 14001:2004 and BS 18001:2007. Those accreditations are a testament to quality, the environment and health and safety.

Dunston's is keen that the skills learned by its skilled craftspeople over the decades are not lost and consequently invests in young people with six further apprentices recently appointed. Employing apprentices ensures the continuation of excellent workmanship through the training and mentoring of young employees which will enable Dunston to build on its excellence reputation long into the future.

The company is now run and owned by two former apprentices - Richard Bourne (who started at Globe Engineering who previously ran the drydock) and Dave Clark (who started at Richard Dunston Hessle Limited).

Dunston's took over the running of William Wright Dry Dock in 1994, renaming the company Dunston (Ship Repairs) Limited.

Europa Crown Ltd
A world leader in oilseed processing equipment

Engineering excellence has propelled Europa Crown into a company known around the world in its specialised field. From its headquarters in Livingstone Road, next to the world famous Humber Bridge, it has built an enviable reputation in the design, supply and start-up of oilseed processing and edible oil refining equipment.

Visitors to the Hessle premises, can be forgiven for thinking the company is much older than it is. The claim above the door states Crown 1878, reality is a little different. Europa Crown actually dates back to 1990 and is based in offices on the banks of the River Humber and has been for the major period of its existence.

When Europa Crown came about it was all about sourcing equipment and project managing the installation and commissioning of that equipment. This was to be achieved by working with Crown Iron Works Inc. based in Minneapolis, USA. The four people who kicked off the Europa Crown business had previous experience of working with Crown Iron over many years whilst working with another business based in the UK. The new association started in the early 1990s and resulted in Crown Iron taking a minority stake in the share capital of Europa Crown. Thus Europa Crown adopted the Crown logo incorporating the 1878 banner.

Above: *Europa Crown Headquarters.* ***Below:*** *Extractor fabrication sections assembled.*

Crown Iron, like Europa Crown, was a private 'family' business. From the beginning of the 1990s through to 2002 Europa Crown built up its business as a majority owned UK Company. With the continued growth of the business, Crown Iron acquired the whole of the share capital and thus we became the European operations of the Crown family business.

After significant growth from the start of the new millennium it was clear to the Crown family that further change was needed and in 2007 CPM Holdings Inc. became the new owners of the Crown businesses. We continue to thrive under their ownership.

The company's success can be attributed to a range of qualities which, when combined, produce the ability to execute projects ranging from the supply of the smallest capacity machine through to the implementation of large semi-turnkey operations, all managed with the same attention to detail.

Europa Crown has continually demonstrated its ability to tailor its scope of supply to meet the precise needs of individual customers. Particular attention is given to working with the appropriate technology and scale of operation for each client as the correct decisions at this stage will ensure the long-term success of the project.

Crown is the world leader in the preparation and extraction industry. Clients include all the major international processors, regional brands and indeed small operators. In association with Sister Companies much of the equipment that the industry requires to extract and process the oil and meal can be sourced from us.

The term generally used as a description of the company's activities reads "the management and implementation of projects to install edible oil and biodiesel production plants". This may require us to supply a single piece of equipment or more usually, a full plant to include layout designs as well as equipment specifications, procurement, shipment, installation and finally commissioning.

The plant designs centre on the processing 'seed' to produce edible oils and probably the best example we can give is via your weekly

grocery shopping. Amongst the many things on a family shopping list will be cooking oil. The oil we typically use when frying our chips and other foodstuffs or adding to other ingredients when preparing meals in the kitchen at home.

Above: *Loading for shipment of a cooker section.* ***Below:*** *A typical gearbox.*

In addition to recovering the oil from seed, at the end of the process we also have what is known as 'Meal'. Meal can be summarised as the leftovers of the seed processing but which has a further use, particularly for feed with farm animals. The Meal is high in proteins and therefore ideally suited to feedstock.

The primary seeds used for the extraction of oil are Rape seed, Sunflower seed and Soyabeans. Rape seed is also known as Canola, mainly in the Americas. Many of you will be familiar with Rape seed though possibly never realised it. Rape is a crop that is grown extensively in many parts of the UK and as nature takes its course following planting, we can all see many acres of yellow flowering fields as we drive along country roads.

Above: Unloading of an extractor section in Germany.

A day in the life of Sam Soybean

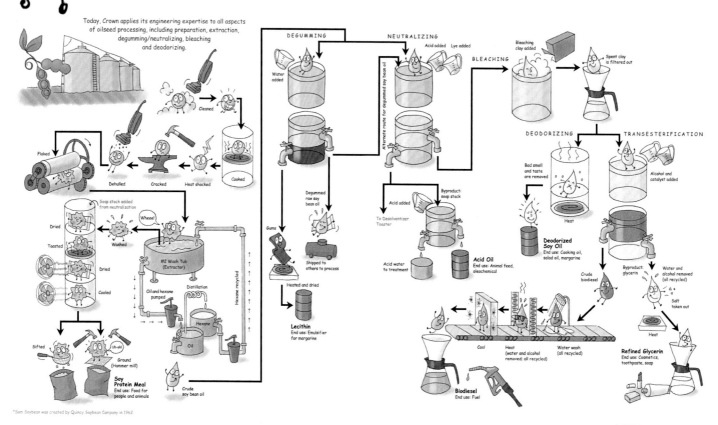

*Sam Soybean was created by Quincy Soybean Company in 1962

A CPM Company

As we move across Europe, the further east we travel the more we will see sunflower growing, a crop extensively grown in areas like Ukraine and Russia for example.

Soyabeans are the primary crop for the Americas although Canola (rape seed) is a key crop most notably in Canada. There is a cartoon like character known as Sam Soybean opposite. This cartoon offers the reader a lighthearted step by step guide to a typical oil extraction process. Sam is in his 70s now but still offers a simple way of explanation of the processes involved.

When we look at the capacity of daily production we see huge variances of output across the world. The range of seed processed can be in the range of 250 tonnes per day to current design capacity of almost 12,000 tonnes per day of seed. Testament to the equipment design is the fact that our machines run for 24 hours a day, 7 days a week with only an occasional shut down for preventative maintenance, usually one or two weeks a year. The higher capacity processing plants are seen in Argentina and Brazil both huge growing areas for Soyabeans. Here in Europe we see all three seeds in production with the largest single machine plant running at around 4,500 tonnes per day.

Over the years Europa Crown has acquired international recognition in the design, supply and commissioning of oilseed processing plants, incorporating preparation, extraction and refining processes in association with Crown Iron Works, our sister company.

Above: Lifting of equipment during site assembly. ***Below left:*** *Part of the Europa Crown team at a company event.*

The sales team covers all of Europe incorporating Russian Federation and down to South Africa capturing the Middle East and India too. A wide and very diverse range of territories with 95% of our sales for the export markets. Locally we have two companies involved with processing seed or oil and over on the Lancashire coast are two further plants and finally one south of London in Kent.

Dedicated project managers keep operations on timetable, using their skills for effective management and liaison with our clients and engineering teams control the installation process for maximum turnaround to hand over an operational plant.

The staff at Europa Crown are highly qualified people, who demonstrate their commitment to the company each and every day. Whilst the business is a part of a much larger group today they have managed to maintain the 'family' feel of the business just as it was back in 1878.

E.W. Brown & Son Ltd
Family-run funeral directors since 1903

Few businesses in the Hull area could claim to have the same emotional bond with the community as E. W. Brown & Son Ltd.

Thousands of families have turned to the company at times of severe grief after losing loved ones, and they have received the highest standards of care from the family-run business.

It has been in the family since formation in 1903 and whilst it has adapted to the practical changes of funerals, the emotional support and quality service provided has remained at the highest standard throughout.

Being family-run and anchored in the community, E. W. Brown & Son Ltd, has been free to operate in the best interests of its clients without having conflicting pressures imposed by out-of-town managements.

This support for the bereaved is much valued with several generations of families continuing to turn to the company in their hours of need.

That is just what Ernest William Brown would have wanted when he founded the business back in 1903. It was his chosen choice of career after earlier being apprenticed into the family business of ship repairers.

He set up in business in Waterloo Street determined to offer a caring and efficient service to build-up his business. His noble horses, magnificent in their polished livery, soon became a familiar sight on the city streets.

Ernest was a well-known character and a sportsman who loved his home city. He did what he could to bring about improvements to the lives of its citizens during the early 20th century.

*Top: Ernest William Brown, who founded the business in 1903. **Above:** A E.W. Brown hearse, circa 1925.*

Above: Mrs Sarah Brown, wife of EW Brown, removes the first piece of turf for the new Craven Park, 1921.

He was a city councillor working without payment on behalf of others, and was heavily connected with Hull Kingston Rovers Rugby League Club, having previously played with local rivals Hull Rugby League Football Club.

For many years he was the club chairman at Hull KR and in 1922 he was largely responsible for the opening of the first Craven Park ground on Holderness Road in September of that year.

Alongside his busy schedule in the city he was also busy building a growing business taking the strain of funeral arrangements off bereaved families.

In 1934 the business moved from Waterloo Street to its present site on Beverley Road. Ernest's son, Eric, was already working in the business at this time and eventually succeeded his father as the leading figure in the firm. In turn, he was succeeded by daughter Angela's husband, Alexander Holland in 1990. Alexander had joined the firm in 1967 and brought additional expertise to the bus-iness when he took over from his father-in-law.

Right: HKR Chairman E.W. Brown with the Yorkshire Cup, 1921.
Below: EW Brown officially opening Craven Park Stadium, Holderness Road in 1922.

Above and inset: Two funerals conducted by the firm.

New family members continued to join the business, Angela and Alexander's son, Gary Holland is celebrating his 40th year in the business. His wife, Christina joined in 2006. David Hill, son-in-law of Chris and Gary joined in 2010 and their daughter Leanne has been working in the business since 1999. Leanne and David are the fifth generation in the business.

Investment in E. W. Brown & Son Ltd across the business has continued, and the latest new fleet of vehicles are now in service. Modernisation of the premises and a full refurbishment of the private chapel have also taken place.

The ethos of the founder has remained intact through the decades which has helped the business thrive when many others have failed or become snapped-up by bigger competitors.

Compassion, care and efficiency are at the forefront of the management and staff dealings' with clients who aren't faced with pushy sales pitches at such an emotional and difficult time.

Instead, they are gently guided through the options with regard to the type and style of services and special requests which are best suited to their wishes.

Many families have commented that Brown's helped them to celebrate the life of loved ones, rather than be completely consumed with grief.

Everything surrounding funerals can be offloaded onto the company which will work to meet the needs of clients.

The modern chapel of rest is supported by a fleet of Mercedes, a hearse and limousines maintained to the highest standards, and for those who wish to turn back the clock, a horse drawn carriage can be arranged, or even a motorcycle or other modes of transport.

Assistance is given with regard to the order of service, floral tributes and venues for refreshments after funerals to ensure everything is taken care of.

The business even has a unique Newland Oak Veneered Coffin which was designed by Ernest's son, Eric. It is suitable for burials and cremations and is of excellent quality. Other options are available such as eco-friendly coffins, specially designed options or American caskets.

The company can also recommend a monumental service which takes away the hassle of dealing with other companies at what is a very difficult time.

Publication of notices in local papers is also taken care of and a spacious private lounge is made available for clients for meetings with family members and ministers. A selection of keepsake urns for cremated remains are also available to view in the lounge.

With the cost of funeral arrangements a concern for many people, alongside a wish of some people to have input into their own funeral, pre-paid funerals have become increasingly popular in recent years. E. W. Brown & Son offer guidance and advice on pre-paid funerals to those who wish to consider that option.

The benefits of having a pre-paid funeral plan include the peace of mind for family members as the funeral will be tailored to an individual's needs or the family's wishes. The funeral director costs are also guaranteed. The money is invested to keep pace with rising costs.

E. W. Brown & Son promise to be available at all hours of need. It offers a 24-hour service, 365 days a year and will always be available to answer your call and you will never be transferred to a call centre. The preferred method of contact is by telephone as is fitting for the high personal service given.

To ensure the highest standard of service at all times, E. W. Brown & Son, is a member of The National Society of Allied and

Left: Eric Ernest Brown, the founder's son, who joined the firm in 1925.

Independent Funeral Directors (SAIF) which is committed to overseeing only the highest standards.

SAIF has been overseeing independent funeral directors since 1989. Back in the old days there weren't such organisations around and it was down to Ernest to set the standards and if is looking down on the business today he will be proud that they have been maintained by successive generations of his family who are successfully driving the business forward and adapting to modern demands.

Traditional hymns are now played alongside pop songs which are chosen as tokens of musical memories by loved ones, colourful clothes are sometimes worn to celebrate the lives of family and friends in upbeat services, and a society which nowadays has more ethnic groups than before, brings new customs and practices and they are catered for with the same respect.

The style and nature of funerals might be much changed since the early days of the 20th century, but one important fact remains intact, and that is the service and care given by the proud family-run funeral business which has been serving families in Hull and beyond for more than 100 years.

Above: The top of the range fleet of new motors show how far transport has developed when viewed against the company's horsedrawn hearse used in the 1920s.

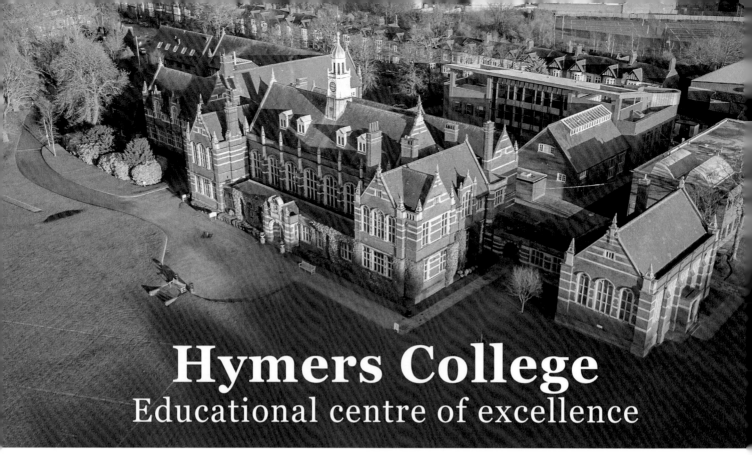

Hymers College
Educational centre of excellence

Ο ne of the north's leading schools will next year celebrate 125 years of education here in Hull.

Hymers College first opened its doors in 1893 as a school for boys on the site of the city's old botanic gardens.

Since then, thousands of boys and girls have received an outstanding education which has been a platform for a successful life for themselves and a benefit to society generally.

Fittingly, for an establishment which has played a significant role in the region, it is an official Venue Partner for the "Back To Ours" festivals in honour of Hull's "City of Culture" year, during

*Top: An aerial photograph of Hymers College. **Below:** The original intake of pupils at Hymers College in 1893.*

HYMERS
COLLEGE

which it will host events and engage further with the community.

Like many long-established schools it owes its formation to a benefactor. That was Reverend John Hymers, Fellow of St John's College, Cambridge, and Rector of Brandesburton, a village 10 miles north of Hull. His legacy was: "for the training of intelligence in whatever social rank of life may be found among the vast and varied population of the town and port of Hull."

Once open, Hymers College soon became a leading school in the north for its academic, sporting and musical achievements. The school has grown to cater for increasing numbers of students. Today, it is a co-educational independent day school for pupils aged 8 to 18 and was ranked among the top 100 schools in the country in a Sunday Times Parent Power supplement.

There are currently 947 pupils on roll and over 2,500 active members of the Old Hymerian Association.

The first Headmaster was Mr Charles Gore who was admitted to the Headmasters' Conference (HMC), which represents the leading independent schools in the country, and all succeeding headmasters have been members.

The school has never forgotten its founding principles and to this day provides bursaries for pupils of ability whose financial circumstances would deny them a Hymers education. From 1946 Hymers became a Direct Grant school with many pupil fees paid for by the local authority. That scheme was phased out in 1975 and the governors decided the school should then go fully independent rather than part of the comprehensive system that Hull was adopting at that time.

Above: Pupils in the gymnasium in the 1900s.

The outbreak of World War I in 1914 brought with it upheaval. The Lancashire Fusiliers arrived to camp at Hymers and set up their headquarters in the pavilion. War service removed half the masters and over 300 Old Hymerians served in the forces.

The horrors of war hit home literally when a bomb dropped by a Zeppelin in 1916 fell in the centre of the running track, leaving a crater six feet deep.

In 1924, a Memorial Hall honouring the fallen in the Great War linked by a corridor to the southern entrance of the main building was completed.

Above: An early photograph of the college with pupils playing in the grounds.

The introduction of the Government-funded Assisted Places scheme in 1980 allowed the school to offer 25 places in each year group to pupils who needed financial support, and when that scheme was abolished in 1997 the Governors decided that bursaries would be provided from the school's resources so that the wishes of its founder could be maintained.

With the start of World War II Hymers College was evacuated by train – 220 seniors and 20 masters and their wives travelled to Pocklington. The 100 juniors went to Market Weighton. A detachment of the RAF (Balloon Barrage Section) established themselves in the college grounds.

But, by December 1939, it was decided to partly re-open Hymers College after air-raid shelters had been provided for 200 people. They were positioned on the ground floor of the new junior wing which had opened a few years earlier.

German bombing left two bomb craters in the college grounds. As war raged metal was in short supply, the ornamental gates and

Hymers College currently spends around 11% of its turnover financing bursaries with over 135 students benefitting from some sort of funding. The newly launched initiative "The Reverend John Hymers Bursary Fund" will allow, over the long term, to substantially increase the funding available for bursaries.

Below: A class studying in the library.

Throughout the school's history it has continued to develop its facilities and learning resources. When plans were submitted in 1907 for a two-storey science building with a corridor bridge to the upper floor, both staff and pupils were delighted that unlike the old building it would have electric lights and central heating!

railings at Hymers were taken away as scrap metal in 1941. They were not replaced until 1949.

Teaching had been split between Hull and Pocklington until 1943 when the school was reunited.

Out-of-school activities continued to be developed and parent-inspired fundraising began in the early 1960s to help the boat club, the music society and provide a minibus for small specialist expeditions and sports teams. Through concerts, social events and successful garden parties, £75,000 in cash and covenants had been raised by 1962 with a further £5,000 promised.

The 1960s also saw the school abolish the cane, a decision which didn't go down well with everybody but there were no complaints from the pupils!

Above: A photograph of pupils taken in 1952.

Above: Hymers College Masters in 1902. **Right:** A school assembly around the 1900s.

In 1971, John Ashurst was appointed Headmaster, and he was in charge during a period of educational change. He successfully steered the school during difficult challenges which included the withdrawal of the direct grant status. 1971 was also the year the school welcomed its first female pupil at Hymers, a former Beverley High School student entered the Sixth Form in preparation for the Oxbridge examinations.

The Junior School during this time increased its number of boys from 125 to 200 and the senior school had 600 pupils. Sports provision now included four rugby and two soccer pitches, three cricket squares, five hard tennis courts, two squash courts, two Eton Fives courts, a miniature rifle range, gymnasium and cricket pavilion.

In 1976 the Governors launched an appeal to strengthen the finances of the school after the direct grant status had been withdrawn and £120,000 was raised. The late seventies and early

eighties saw junior school soccer pitches built on reclaimed land. In addition, a large sports hall was built with an indoor tennis court, four badminton courts, indoor five-a-side football pitch, basketball pitch and indoor cricket nets.

Mr Ashurst retired in 1983 and Bryan Bass took over as Headmaster and set about further refurbishment of the college buildings. In 1987 a physics lecture room was opened and No. 83 Hymers Avenue was converted into offices which is now home to finance, marketing and operations, along with the school shop. Another major development of the Bass years was the construction of the design centre. His final building project was the conversion of the old armoury block into new music rooms.

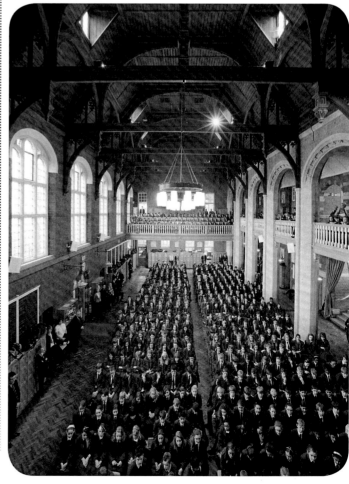

*Recent developments: In September, 2014, The Stephen Martin Music School (**above left**) was opened by John Rutter and The Learning Resource Centre (**Above right**) was opened by Tim Waterstone in April 2016.*

Whilst the first female pupil attended back in 1971 it was not until 1989 – after two failed attempts – a decision was made to admit girls. On the first day of school term that September there were 919 pupils of which 788 were boys and 131 girls. By 1991 there were girls at every level of the school.

In 1980 John Morris was appointed Head of History before progressing to Deputy Head in 1986 and then in 1990 he took over from Bryan Bass as Headmaster. He oversaw developments including the opening in 1995 of the Judi Dench Theatre by the actress herself. In 2000 additional land was purchased next to the railway lines and an Astroturf was completed in 2002. The new Sixth-Form Centre and the swimming pool were opened in 2003.

In 2006 David Elstone became Headmaster following the retirement of Mr Morris. Since then, Mr Elstone has actively built stronger links with the local community and hosted events such as the Disability Games, Kwik Cricket Tournaments and Humber Games with local state schools.

The school is proud of its association with the local homeless charity Emmaus Hull and continues to host a variety of events throughout the year in order to donate the proceeds to the charity.

Above: *Pupils singing at the annual Christmas Carol Concert.*
Above centre: *Headmaster Mr David Elstone.*

The most popular event is the annual Christmas Carol Concert which raises upwards of £5,000.

Recent developments at Hymers include the Stephen Martin Music School which was opened by John Rutter in September 2014. It has music technology and rehearsal rooms on the first floor; a large rehearsal room, band room, and fully equipped state-of-the art recording studio on the second floor. It also includes sound proofed percussion rooms and seven individual teaching and practice rooms.

The Learning Resource Centre was opened by Tim Waterstone in April 2016, which had been a long-term ambition of Mr Elstone. When he was first interviewed in May 2005 he was asked what was missing from the facilities at Hymers. He replied "a library" and since his appointment he and the Governors have worked towards building the Learning Resource Centre. To keep a piece of the school's history intact, the "old gym" was maintained during the new build and the space is often used for assemblies, internal examinations and other events.

Although located in the city centre, the school has seen its catchment area stretch from Bridlington to Lincolnshire, to Howden and Withernsea.

The school's aim is to enable all pupils to achieve outstanding academic qualifications, as well as offering extensive extra-curricular activities, which encourages pupils to develop their talents to the full.

"We believe a good education should inspire boys and girls to take every opportunity offered by a school to develop their talents. Hymers College is full of motivated, happy pupils who are doing just that," said Mr Elstone.

"We pride ourselves on the quality and breadth of the curriculum we provide whilst also developing the creative, sporting and personal skills of all our pupils. We are a school that welcomes progress in education but also cherishes traditional values."

Neill & Brown Global Logistics
100 years on the clock and still motoring along

The impending growth of motorised transport and Hull's strategic location led to the formation of one of Britain's most respected logistics providers.

Neill & Brown was established in the city in 1917, after a chat in a pub between an Englishman and an Irishman, who saw past the traditional horse and cart used to transport timber from Hull docks, and into the future potential open to them on the roads.

That vision has been built on by subsequent company leaders, and the result is an innovative business that has grasped new opportunities and gained an enviable reputation for its level of service and commitment to clients, who now benefit from a modern fleet of fuel efficient eco-friendly vehicles.

Today, integrated supply-chain solutions are provided and supported by a successful track record in domestic and global markets. This includes expertise in transportation, abnormal loads, warehousing documentation, packaging and insurance.

*Above: Moving caravans in the early years. **Below:** Colin Moody, Managing Director (left) and Peter Brown, C.E.O. of Neill & Brown.*

The business offers numerous secure, daily timed collections and deliveries, tailored for a wide range of products, from food ingredients, packaging, machine equipment and general cargoes, to chemicals, hazardous and specialist loads.

Neill & Brown believes it offers unmatched management of the flow of resources between the point of origin and the point of destination. Using staff expertise and the latest technology support it guarantees customers are kept informed of progress throughout the distribution process, and they are reassured that their products are secure at the central hub which has gated security and CCTV surveillance.

In the early days, the business was only involved in transporting timber imported from Scandinavian countries, but it now has an impressive track record of development and innovation which has ensured it can look forward to the next 100 years.

During World War Two from 1939 to 1945 the company played an important part in the war effort supplying provisions for the British Army, and later became involved in the region's highly successful caravan industry specialising in the movement of abnormal loads by road throughout the UK and Europe.

Above: Neill & Brown serves a large number of international customers thanks to its warehouse based near the Port of Hull. *Below:* Neill & Brown are experts at moving specialist loads.

Continued investment and expansion has elevated turnover into the millions and the company is now operating around the world with a strong presence in both developed and emerging markets. Business is growing in the United States, India, and the Far East through a Hong Kong office and Far East agents.

1990 saw the company relocated into new headquarters at Livingstone Road, Hessle, adjacent to the Humber Estuary, the E20 corridor and the city's rail and road networks.

In 2011, the company joined forces with Nippon Gohsei in a major development of new laboratory, manufacturing, storage and distribution facilities at Marfleet Environmental Industries Park

in East Hull – a site that is ideal due to its proximity to the Port of Hull. In 2014, a second warehouse was opened at the park to serve a growing number of customers.

The main markets are the UK and Europe, and the company's easily recognisable fleet of vehicles moves through countries including Italy, Belgium, Germany, Holland, France, Denmark, Spain and Switzerland on a daily basis.

Staff numbers have grown to around 130 at the family owned business, and the latest operating systems are in place to ensure efficiency as the company continues to seek new opportunities. The new transit warehouse in Hessle was custom made for the

company's double-decker trailers and the loading and unloading of pallets. This is a growing area of the business which can now handle pallets as efficiently as possible and that service is now fully integrated into the suite of logistic services offered by Neill & Brown.

As in any competitive market, cost is a major consideration, and Neill & Brown always ensures its 40-strong fleet is operated at optimum efficiency to maintain the company reputation for reliability and getting goods delivered at the right place at the right time.

The fleet is predominantly Volvo and DAF and is changed on a five-year cycle. In addition to that, the company is keen to stay ahead of statutory requirements and proactively upgrades its vehicles in order to reduce its carbon footprint, and operates a fleet that is more efficient and greener than the competition. This continual major investment is testament that the company takes its responsibilities seriously.

Those responsibilities are also evident among the driving team. They are all highly trained and fully adept and qualified in the safe loading and rapid handling of high volume, highly valuable cargo. A number of our drivers are trained in the handling of hazardous goods and chemical cargoes.

Neill & Brown also teamed up with one of its clients, Orvec International, to help improve road safety. It has equipped its fleet with a unique emergency thermal blanket made in Hull by Orvecare, a division of Orvec International. The Orve+Wrap blanket captures a person's heat and uses thermal pockets to create convection heat to raise, then maintain, core temperature. It has twice the thermal TOG rating of a typical summer duvet that will alleviate hypothermia and maintain normothermia.

The blankets can be used to keep drivers warm and dry in any breakdown situation, and as professional drivers are often first on the scene at accidents, they could offer support until help arrives. The two companies have worked together for more than 10 years with Neill & Brown providing about 90 per cent of Orvec International's logistics and transport needs around the UK, Europe and the Far East.

Neill & Brown is currently headed by chief executive Peter Brown – who is the third generation of his family at the helm – and he has been with the company for over 50 years.

He has overseen the rapid expansion of recent years and put the company on a sound footing for further growth with the infrastructure developments and overseas connections.

Having seen business growth during the early recessionary years of this century, he expects rising demand for the wide-ranging quality logistic services on offer.

*Top: Steve Moran operating a crane mounted truck which is capable of lifting units of up to nine tonnes. **Left:** From the left, are Tony Codd from Orvecare, Glenn Cartwright, driver for Neill & Brown, and Colin Moody, Neill & Brown MD with the Orve+Wrap thermal blanket.*

Above: *Logistics director Carl Andrew with the new vehicle livery celebrating Neill & Brown's 100 years.*

Mr Bown is proud that many of the staff, like himself, have had a long association with the business stretching back decades. His first major job when he started in 1965, after being the office boy, was palletising imported Scandinavian timber at the former RAF Catfoss airfield in East Yorkshire for onward distribution.

He went through the ranks to managing director and then his current role and his wide experience has included responsibility for customs documentation and caravan transportation.

Right: *Moira Brown with a Hamper of a centenary truck full of 'Hullness'.*

Mr Brown has always ensured Neill & Brown is active in its local community – it was the first local business to sign up as a Hull Angel with a £17,000 commitment in support of the City of Culture 2017 – and has a record of backing business organisations and charities.

The company's celebrations to mark its proud 100-year history were kick-started with hampers of "Hullness." Fun cardboard models of the firm's centenary trucks were distributed to long-standing customers. In support of Made in Hull, the theme for the first quarter of Hull 2017, the hampers were packed with products that had been made in the city which included food and art.

Throughout 2017 Neill & Brown also have planned events paying homage to the people that have made the company and the city the successes that they are.

"It's a happy coincidence that our centenary year coincides with Hull 2017. It's an opportunity to further increase the profile of our business, celebrate the contribution of staff, and thank our customers," said Mr Brown.

169

Alan Wood & Partners
50 years of technical and professional expertise

The 1960s was a period of rapid change in the construction industry as the old longhand methods of calculations by log tables and slide rules were being replaced by electronic devices.

There was also a growing need for expert civil and structural consultants for the increasing number of highly technical projects in the pipeline.

Alan Wood & Partners was formed in 1968 to provide that expertise and is now recognised as a market leading civil and structural engineering consulting service suited for large and small projects.

In those early days the first computers were out of reach financially and the business had to "hire time" from outside companies for detailed structural analysis.

Above: *Current directors and associates of Alan Wood & Partners.*

Eventually, as the practice grew, computers were purchased for design analysis alongside equipment for "draughting" capability to keep all work "in-house."

The move to metrication also brought challenges as that affected all areas of work from building materials to office equipment.

Regulations within the industry were constantly changing and severe gale damage which affected the UK in the early years prompted changes to the wind loading calculations in building design.

Above: *Early days: The original directors and associates.*
Bottom: *Alan Wood meets HRH Queen Elizabeth.*

European Codes of Practice also had an effect on design approaches and had to be a consideration in all projects.

Investment in technology by the practice has been ongoing and it now benefits from the improvements in technology the latest high-tech equipment brings.

Alan Wood & Partners now has the benefit of a significant technical staff resource and ongoing training ensures they are conversant with current standards in the latest Codes of Practice.

Full professional management and engineering design services are offered to clients which starts with the initial feasibility and concept studies through to delivery and operation of facilities.

For each project, the practice uses a team of the most suited personnel working under the guidance of a director. Emphasis is placed on flexibility in solving design and site problems as well as working within schedules and cost constraints.

The practice holds accreditations to ISO 9001, ISO 14001, CHAS, Constructionline, Achilles Link-up and CATCH.

Left: Allam Medical Building at the University of Hull Below: 3D Image of the new bakery and juice factory in Saudi Arabia. Bottom: The Gosschalks Solicitors building.

It is active across a wide range of sectors and major construction projects in the UK and abroad.

Early local projects in Hull include the towering tanks for Anglia Oils Ltd, at King George Dock; The Salvation Army Hostel, the administration buildings for The Humber Bridge Board; and in north Lincolnshire the new wharf and cargo handling facilities for Associated Waterways Services Ltd. More recent projects include the regional BBC Headquarters in Queens Gardens, C4DI building and amphitheatre and the Allam Medical Building.

Clients include many national companies and public authorities and the numbers continue to grow as does the practice. It was originally based at Bishop Lane, Hull, but following rapid expansion moved to larger premises at Beverley Road, Hull, in 1976. The adjoining property was acquired in 1983 and refurbishment completed in 1985. There are now also offices in Lincoln, London, Manchester, Scarborough, Sheffield and York.

With roots and a head office based on the UK's energy estuary in Hull, Alan Wood & Partners is providing expertise across a wide range of technical and professional services to the renewables and energy sectors. These are diverse and far reaching in what is an embryonic and fast growing sector. They range from high level strategic and economic input at concept stage through to detailed planning, development and delivery of projects. The client base includes investors, producers, generators and users of energy.

The full range of energy and renewables sources and technologies services cover: Downstream hydrocarbon production, energy from waste, on and offshore wind, solar, biomass, ground source, distribution, infrastructure and facilities.

With demand for energy continually growing Alan Wood & Partners is working with its partners to reduce the pressure on natural resources and the environment and is confident its technical ability, combined with pragmatic solutions will deliver results.

The practice celebrates its 50th anniversary next year and it's staggering to consider the changes it has encountered during that time, and the ability it has shown to prosper and grow in all areas of the construction industry.

No one in the early days could have predicted the move from long hand calculations would lead to such highly technical solutions being developed by the practice, which would bring benefits for clients, the public and the environment well into the 21st century.

Associated British Ports
Port of Hull

ABP is the UK's largest port operating company, managing 21 ports around Britain and handling almost 100 million tonnes of cargo every year. ABP's ports include four ports on the Humber estuary: Goole, Grimsby, Hull and Immingham.

The Humber is the UK's busiest trading estuary with around 30,000 vessel movements every year and ABP's ports are a key part of this trade, handling in excess of £75 billion worth of goods every year. The Port of Hull is one of the biggest ports in the UK in its own right and contributes £538 million to the local economy, in turn supporting around 8,000 local jobs.

The Port of Hull has been transformed since it's opening in 1778 when it was known to be the first commercial quay built on the Humber. The port has handled every conceivable type of cargo and has had to remain adaptable to being able to handle larger shipments, new commodities and to continually meet customer needs.

Three years ago saw the King George Dock centenary celebrations take place at the Port of Hull. Built in June 1914, the development became suspended when when World War 1 broke out two days after his Majesty King George the fifth, accompanied by her Majesty Queen Mary officially opened the dock.

When King George Dock first opened, it was dominated by coal exports but now, the largest operation within the dock is freight and cruise ferry passengers, with Hull being the fourth largest port for international ferry passengers in the UK, handling around 1 million passengers a year.

The Port of Hull is the UK's leading softwood timber port and combined with the Port of Immingham, the two handle around 1

Above: *Fully enclosed, Hull All Weather Terminal.*
Photograph: *David Lee Photography Ltd/ABP.*

million tonnes of timber a year. The port benefits from specialist terminals dedicated to handling key cargoes and is also the focus of the Humber's burgeoning renewable energy sector.

Hull All Weather Terminal (HAWT) is the UK's largest and only fully-enclosed terminal which is specially designed to handle weather sensitive cargoes such as steel and forest products. HAWT's specialist overhead cranes have the ability to discharge a vessel at 80 lifts per hour and benefits from multimodal interconnectivity, meaning that a train can be loaded with steel coil, whilst a vessel is simultaneously being discharged.

Opened in May 2000, the Finland Terminal was built at a cost of £6 million to accommodate softwood timber import volumes from Northern Europe, the Baltic States and Scandinavia. The Finland

Above: *Double decker buses being exported from the Port of Hull.* ***Above right:*** *Bundles of wool being discharged.*
Photographs: *Rob J Bell.*

Above: Hull Container Terminal.　　　　　　　　　　**Photograph:** *Karl Andre Photography Ltd/ABP.*

Terminal offers over 60,000 sq m of covered accommodation for the storage of paper, pulp and panel products from Finland and represents the North of UK hub for the Finnish forest products industry.

Hull Container Terminal, which is currently undergoing an infrastructural transformation, is a pivotal part of the business on the Humber designed to support the increase in capacity for containerised goods. The terminal recently benefitted from a £15 million investment boost from ABP which saw two Liebherr ship to shore gantry cranes being delivered, increasing productivity and enabling a higher rate of lifts per hour.

Above: Transforming infrastructure, The Green Port Hull project.
Photograph: *David Lee Photography Ltd/ABP.*

In Hull, ABP are at the forefront of the renewable energy sector. The Green Port Hull project with Siemens is transforming existing port infrastructure into a world class advanced manufacturing facility, securing the Humber's role as the nation's energy estuary.

This £310 million investment (of which £150 million was invested by ABP) by both ABP and Siemens is acting as a catalyst for economic growth and development in the region.

The project involved the regeneration of Alexandra Dock in Hull in order to establish an offshore wind turbine manufacturing and assembly facility for Siemens. This will be complemented by a rotor blade manufacturing site near Paull to the east of the port estate.

An additional renewable energy commodity is wood pellet, also known as biomass. Hull's rail load out facility was built to supply the UK's largest power station Drax who recently converted three of its six generators to become a predominantly biomass fuelled station.

The facility which was completed in 2014 and boasts a 49m high concrete silo as well as an intricate network of conveyors, designed to handle the fragile cargo. The facility can load 1,500 tonnes of biomass in 40 minutes and handles 1 millions tonnes of biomass every year.

With variations in trends across the different commodities being imported and exported, ABP remains vigilant and willing to adapt current ways of working to ensure the customer's needs are put first and to keep Britain trading.

Above (left to right): *The founders of the Beverley Building Society are, Mr. F. Hall, Mr T. G. Johnson, Mr Jas. Mills, Mr. G. Welburn and Mr. J. H. Hewson.*

Beverley Building Society
A strong independent mutual

Based at 57 Market Place, Beverley Building Society was founded in 1866 by Mr James Mills, Mr F. Hall, Mr T. G. Johnson, Mr G. Welburn and Mr J. H. Hewson, as the Beverley Permanent Building Society.

The purpose of the Society, defined in its 1875 rules was: "To enable its members to purchase land, or to build or purchase one or more dwelling houses or other real or leasehold property, according to his interest in the Society and that such interest shall be in shares of £60 each, half shares of £30, and quarter shares in £15 value, and that either males or unmarried females, if of age, may become members of the Society."

In 1866, there were a total of 93 members, generating £406 in subscriptions, in 2016 the Society report 13,000 savings accounts and 1500 mortgages, with total assets of £192m.

2016 marked the beginning of the Society's 150th Anniversary, the celebrations were a thanks to the people in the local community,

Above: *Society staff raising money for Action Duchenne by having a bake sale at the Beverley Food Festival, which is sponsored by the Society.* ***Below left:*** *Staff and board of directors at the 150th Anniversary dinner.*

and to the many previous and present staff, for helping the Society to support the local area for a century and a half.

Despite being in business for 150 years, the Society retains the ethos that has been in place since founding: to be a strong, independent mutual which is trusted and respected by members and non-members, offering straightforward, value for money products that are easy to understand, and are supported by an unrivalled level of personal service.

Above: The Beverley Building Society - a view from Lairgate. *Below:* The revised logo for the Society for the 150th Anniversary.

The Society hosted a 150th Anniversary dinner, which had over 200 invitees, consisting of members, staff, and associates and for the duration of 2016/17, the Society had a charity partner - Action Duchenne – the staff skydived, ran half marathons and zip wired to raise over £25,000 for the charity. The Society also supports local charities and community events throughout the year.

Continuing the 150th celebrations, the Society is to bury a Time Capsule at the end of the anniversary year in June 2017. The Society has appealed on local radio stations and TV for locals to suggest or donate items for the time capsule, which is to contain memorabilia from the Society such as the infamous money boxes and various historic documents. The capsule to be dug up 50 years from burial.

The Society is dedicated to being a strong independent mutual society, offering a 'life cycle' portfolio of savings and mortgage products, including helping people looking to purchase their first home. In 2016 Beverley Building Society won the Mortgage Finance Gazette 'Best Local Building Society' award for innovative and consistently competitive mortgage products offered nationally, with excellent customer service.

The Society supports many local events throughout the year, every year; Beverley Food Festival, Beverley Folk Festival, Driffield Show, and Beverley Literature Festival. In addition to contributing to the continuation of local festivals, the Society is a sponsor of the East Riding Theatre and Beverley Rugby Club.

Left: The Society trailer at the 2016 Driffield show, which is sponsored by the Society.

Broady Flow Control
Innovative and Effective solutions

Like many local businesses Broady Flow Control has its roots based on Hull Docks and was formed at a time when it was the biggest fishing port in the British Empire, and provided food and materials for a third of Britain.

That was back in 1902 when William Broady, a coppersmith by trade, decided to set-up his own company and take advantage of the booming port.

In the early days much of the company's work involved installing and repairing marine pipework on the local trawler fleet.

By the early 1930s Broady had expanded its operations and was manufacturing a range of valves and cocks, including reducing valves for larger boilers which were installed in trawlers at that time.

This became an important part of the business and to accommodate demand, a new department was set up specifically to manufacture pressure reducing and safety relief valves which became the core of Broady Flow Control.

Above: How it used to be: Early 20th century fabrications ready for despatch.

Today, Broady Flow Control is a world leading specialist valve manufacturing company and it has been a key supplier to the Royal Navy since 1938 which led to the Broady Naval division being developed for both the UK and international markets.

Broady Naval continues to extend its supply into new areas and applications in the defence industry, having already supplied the Royal Navy's Type 45 Destroyer, Astute Class Submarine, AO, LPD, LPH programmes and in addition to supporting current worldwide naval in-service requirements.

Above: Company premises back in the 1960s. Below: A fully equipped workshop which has helped staff produce the best quality products at any given time.

Broady Flow Control has built its reputation over 100 years on innovation and high quality products which are sought after in a wide range of industries, and they are made from a variety of materials including carbon steel, stainless steel, and nickel aluminium bronze.

A complete range of relief and safety valves are supplied to the chemical, petrochemical, oil and gas, power, waste and water, paper and pulp, food, fire protection, mining and pharmaceutical industries.

From premises at English Street, Hull, design and manufacturing expertise is supported by extensive engineering facilities which enable the company to offer a full engineering service to both divisions from in-house design, foundry services and machining, through to assembly and testing to customers' exacting requirements.

Right: A modern display: showcasing the company's naval division at DSEi 2015, London. *Below:* Furnace workers melting metal under controlled conditions.

Broady foundry achieves an enviable quality rate using the latest moulding and melting equipment and techniques alongside certified ingots and melting under controlled conditions. The pattern shop employs skilled staff using quality equipment to interpret customer instructions.

Computer-aided solid modelling is available to predict the casting process which ensures a low scrap rate and keeps costs down. The company has also developed a robust quality management system which supports order processing and manufacturing ensuring the highest standards are maintained at all times throughout the business.

The valves manufactured cover a wide range of conditions and it is important Broady is aware of the conditions on which the valves are to operate to enable it to provide the complete engineering solution.

Safety/Relief valves are installed to automatically prevent a safe pressure being exceeded in fired or unfired pressure vessels or pipeline systems. Reducing valves are installed where it is required to reduce from one level of pressure to another, whilst providing the required fluid flow to satisfy a downstream demand.

Hydrant reducing valves are suitable for firefighting applications where pressure reduction is required. Surplus/sustaining valves are designed to control the upstream pressure and to surplus away liquids or gases so as to recycle rather than waste. Marine valves are a range of high-integrity valves and fittings used by the UK Ministry of Defence and foreign navies worldwide.

Throughout its history, investment in the business has been continuous and in 2010 Broady Flow Control secured its future further when it became part of the Valvitalia Group – an Italian manufacturer of valves and other energy equipment – and the remarkable synergies between the two organisations should lead to a bright future ahead.

Above and right: The memorial stone featuring William Broady's name and the golden statue of King William III in the Market Place. It was raised in 1734 to commemorate the revolution of 1688 when the protestant Dutch King, William of Orange, landed in Devon and deposed the unpopular King James II, thereby inaugurating Britain's constitutional monarchy. Hull is linked as it was taken without bloodshed by protestant supporters thereby allowing the Catholic governor to be removed.

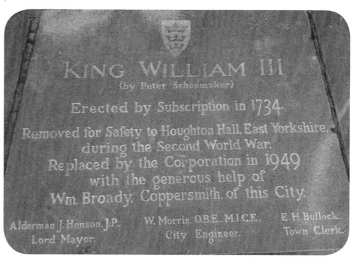

Burstalls Solicitors
Professional Legal Services

For over 70 years Burstalls Solicitors have been working to meet the needs of their clients who benefit from a comprehensive range of legal services delivered by expert lawyers.

The firm initially practised from Imperial Chambers in Bowlalley Lane, and then other premises before moving in 1979 into its present impressive Grade II location at Ocean Chambers, 54 Lowgate, Hull.

The site has a rich history and once formed part of the Suffolk Palace which was built in approximately 1387 by Sir Michael De La Pole, who was the Lord Chancellor and Earl of Suffolk.

One of his forebears was Sir William De La Pole who was the first Lord Mayor of Hull and a member of the family of Merchant Princes who did much to increase the prosperity of the port and make its history.

King Henry VIII purchased the manor house and resided there during his visit in 1540 and it was later owned by King Charles I.

Above and left: *Founder, Bryan Burstall.*

Archives reveal that the area on which Ocean Chambers now stands was mostly industrial during the 19th century, and then in 1901 Ocean Chambers in its present state was erected. It was commissioned by the Ocean Accident & Guarantee Corporation Ltd and remains in excellent condition today with a wonderful frontage.

The strong stone façade, is asymmetrical with Baroque touches, including shallow cantered bays divided by squat iconic columns, mannerist gables and a heavy rusticated entrance.

In addition to the large boardrooms on the ground floor at the front of the building, there is an ornate mosaic floor on both the ground floor and basement level. The staircase is of Edwardian construction, but perhaps the most appealing aspect, are the spacious vaults which run under the footprint of the building and under Lowgate.

Prior to the building of the Hull Tidal Barrier, Lowgate used to flood regularly and these vaults were built to be flood proof as well as fire and theft proof.

Burstall Solicitors are proud of the relationship that it has built with its local community and every September hosts Heritage

Open Days to allow the public to see inside this fantastic building. Visitors are given access to the fine labyrinth of passages under the footprint of the building. The internal workings of the safe doors are also open for inspection.

Over 700 people have visited in previous years and more are expected this year - from Thursday, September 7, to Saturday, September 10 - with Hull celebrating its "City of Culture" status.

Ocean Chambers continued to be occupied by The Ocean Accident & Guarantee Corporation Ltd until 1962. It was then occupied by William Brown Atkinson Shipping and Forwarding Agents until Burstalls purchased the premises in 1979.

Burstalls Solicitors was established in 1946 by Bryan Burstall, and his son Patrick Burstall is currently Senior Partner, and the firm has successfully built a reputation for providing high quality, common sense advice.

Patrick specialises in many aspects of Private Client work and is a member of STEP (the worldwide respected Society of Trust and Estate Practitioners). He is also a past President of the Hull Incorporated Law Society and the Hull and Literary and Philosophical Society.

*Above: The impressive exterior of Burstalls Solicitors, Ocean Chambers, Hull. **Below left:** Burstalls' partners are, from left to right: Terry Moore, Patrick Burstall and David Rosenberg.*

Specialist advice is given by Burstalls Solicitors in the following areas: Wills, Trusts and Probate; Lasting Powers of Attorney (LPA) & Court of Protection; Family Law/Divorce; Conveyancing/ Moving House; Employment Law; Civil Litigation; Personal Injury/Accident Claims; Commercial Services/Commercial Property; Agricultural Law.

Clients are given independent and expert legal solutions that are intelligent, cost-effective and clear in the specific area of law relevant to them as soon as they require it.

The client base is predominantly from the Hull and surrounding area but clients are also represented across the UK and abroad, helped by state-of-the-art IT systems which mean distance is not a problem. Every client has a qualified lawyer appointed to deal with their case who is a specialist in that particular field. This enhanced service gives reassurance to clients who avoid being lost in the "system" as can happen with "call-centre" advice.

Anyone requiring the professional legal services offered is encouraged to contact Burstalls for an initial consultation or to fill in an online enquiry form.

Greens the Signmakers Ltd
Excellent relationships with clients

Established in 1963 the company was founded by Reg Green, a time served sign writer who at the age of 42 embarked on a business career that would see sign making develop as a major industry.

Reg took premises in Waterhouse Lane in Hull, a street now dwarfed by the Princes Quay shopping centre. The business took on a joiner to make up the sign panels and later a painter to finish the panels into colour', ready for the sign written lettering. The firm continued to expand and soon there was a busy team making and fitting signs throughout Hull and surrounding areas.

The early 60's saw the first use of Acrylic (Perspex) in the sign industry and Reg saw an opportunity to expand the business and created some of the first back lit signs in Hull. The faces were in opal acrylic with cut out coloured lettering applied for the logo. The signs were illuminated by fluorescent tubes in metal boxes behind the face panels.

Rapid growth followed and new premises were needed. A factory in Clarendon Street was secured and the business continued its growth there for several years. More staff were employed including a production manager for the first time.

Manufacture of the lettering was all done by hand, using an overhead projector to enlarge text to the required size, traced

*Top: Founder, Reg Green 1921-1993. **Above right:** A car showroom with signs manufactured by Greens. **Below and opposite page:** Signs designed and fitted by Greens.*

onto material and then hand cut. This was slow and expensive so a pantograph router was purchased to allow different size lettering to be produced from a single template.

In 1967 Reg's son Stephen joined the firm and helped with the development of the business. At this point the retail superstore concept began to emerge. Cliff Dunn, Savemore, Carlines and Newholme Paints, were all Hull brands that needed bright and effective signs for their new shops.

Newholme paints became 'Status Discount Stores' and branches sprang up in every major city throughout the land. Greens were busy making not only signs but also internal displays for these stores. So busy in fact that another move became essential. Lister Street, off Hessle Road, became the firm's new home.

In 1973 Reg's son Chris joined the firm and worked his way through every department to learn the business. By this time Stephen was MD and Reg had taken more of a back seat. Chris had to learn quickly, as in 1976 Stephen moved to set up another business, leaving Chris to become MD at the age of 21.

The continued surge of Retail Store and Retail Park development brought many new opportunities to the firm and Chris grasped them eagerly. Bigger, brighter and better signs were demanded

so another move in 1984 saw the business in custom built premises of 26,000 sq ft in Brighton Street.

Many new materials, processes and techniques have been introduced over the years. Greens have always embraced new technology and were quickly into the production of Flexible skin signs when they were introduced from America. The system allowed the creation of very large sign boxes using a single flexible skin for the face, tensioned over a light box containing fluorescent tubes. The retailers loved them as their brands could be presented at sizes that could only be dreamt of 5 years before. Greens have produced such signs as big as 20m x 6m deep!!

The early versions of flexible skin signs involved a pre coloured skin and the text had to be masked and eradicated to leave the wording for the sign in white. The process was slow and expensive and was quickly replaced by the use of translucent self adhesive vinyl's cut to designs and applied to plain white skins. Whilst this was a big improvement, the industry continued to search for a more flexible method. At this time Greens were introduced to large format digital printing. Starting on a small scale with a 1200mm wide machine, the team quickly saw the potential of creating full colour photographic images for use in signage. A second and third machine quickly followed taking production capacity up to 2.5m wide.

Chris's son Lawrence joined the business in 2007, having spent school holidays and a gap year working within the company. As the third generation of the family Lawrence brought new energy to the company and has continued the development of its digital capacity. In 2015, he introduced a new printer that could not only print roll materials, but also sheets, and up to a massive 3.2m wide. This facility proved so popular that it has been run on 24 hour shift work at times to cope with demand. The use of digital print has continued in the production of flexible

*Above and inset: Greens offices in Brighton Street and work being printed on a Vutek GS5500LXr Pro. **Below:** Managing Director Chris Green and son Lawrence, Operations Director of Greens.*

skin signs and Lawrence realised they need to go bigger still if they were to keep pace. A Vutek machine was sourced that took capacity up to a massive 5.2m wide and allowed Greens to print multi layer skins for special illuminated effects. Lawrence is now Operations Director at the firm and looks after the day to day running of the business.

Greens have enjoyed the support of its loyal staff throughout its 50+ year history. Some employees even joined as school leavers and stayed until retirement. They currently employ more than 60 people of which ten have more than 30 years service. That's a lot of sign making experience!

The respected clients of Green the Signmakers include a variety of businesses and many high street and retail park stores. Whether you require a nationwide roll-out or a bespoke order, every client receives the same level of care and attention. It is testament to the level of commitment and service demonstrated at Greens, that many of their clients have been regular customers for more than 20 years.

As a family run business, Green's pride themselves on tradition and remaining strong to their original values, while still remaining at the forefront of the signage industry.

Hull Cartridge Company
Unrivalled experience in cartridge design and production

As Hull Cartridge Company Ltd enters its 70th trading year, choose 'Hull' when only the very best shotgun ammunition will do.

Sydney Bontoft formed Hull Cartridge Company Ltd and began making his own cartridges in 1947.

HULL CARTRIDGE
SINCE 1947

The roots of the business go back to the 1920s. Turners Carbides was Sydney's original incorporated business retailing Calcium Carbide to local estates and farms throughout the Hull area. Carbide, when mixed with water, produces acetylene gas, add a naked flame and you get a source of light. As electricity spread throughout the country, Sydney saw the steady demise of the demand for Calcium Carbide and, finding an alternative product, began supplying shotgun cartridges to these customers.

Early cartridge production used the Dixon loading block system which was hand operated. Hull Cartridge was a small business retailing mainly in Northern England. Taking the Three Crowns of Kingston upon Hull, the Company incorporated this into their brand. By the early 1960s, the management team had expanded and now consisted of Sydney, his sons Peter and Ken with Hugh Clark heading up Sales. Mechanisation had come to the forefront and increased volumes of production could easily be achieved.

Above: Ladies hand loading cartridges circa 1950. **Right:** *An advertisement for Weihrauch Rifles which are imported by Hull Cartridge Company.*

From right to left are Ken Sydney and Peter Bontoft outside the company's site at Bontoft Avenue.

Hugh, located in Sussex, soon helped establish the Hull brand. Early success included convincing leading gun-makers Holland & Holland to have their own brand custom loaded by Hull, multiple gun-makers followed ; Hull Cartridge Company was on it's way to establishing a national customer base.

Hull also have another string to their bow. In 1977, they began representing Weihrauch, a little known German airgun manufacturer. In 2017, Hull still represent this product; of course it's another Number 1 brand.

Sales continued to grow and in 1980 the Company moved to a brand new purpose built site located at Bontoft Avenue, Hull.

In the family tradition, Peter's children David and Susan joined the business in 1981. Sydney retired in 1982, happy that another family generation was taking interest.

The demand for shotgun shooting has continued to increase at a pace through the subsequent decades. Corporate entertainment has embraced both clay and game shooting. Shooting grounds continue to improve their facilities giving a better service and experience. Simulated game shooting is the new found fun sport.

The Bontoft family are proud owners of the Hull Cartridge brand: the Number 1 in the eyes of many. In 1992, Hull received a Royal Warrant, 'By Appointment to Her Majesty the Queen', an endorsement of it's quality.

The product line is extensive, with modern classics such as High Pheasant and Sovereign retaining popularity. Whatever your shooting needs, Hull Cartridge have the solution, all of which are showcased on their new website at www.hullcartridge.co.uk. Three Crowns paper cased cartridges are still available, some things change, others remain the same.

With product performance guaranteed, consistent velocity shot after shot, and moderate levels of recoil, the demand for Hull Cartridge is not only nationwide but reaches Europe and Australasia.

Above: Peter's children David and Susan are both directors of the business and enjoy shooting in the field.

A family business, driven by an ambitious and innovative team, determined to deliver excellence in both product and service to an international market place".

David's daughters, the fourth generation, are following in the family tradition. Faye has responsibility for operational issues, her sister Isabel is working with Susan to maintain the Company's high market profile. There are no male Bontoft heirs in the fourth generation, are the family worried?.... An emphatic 'No' is the answer.

Above: *Cartridges on the modern production line.* **Right:** *Three Crowns 12 gauge paper cased cartridges.*

Long standing key members of staff bring experience to a younger, hungry sales team, led by Robert Everitt, whose emphasis on customer support is paramount. Neil Hookem, Factory Manager since 1991, brings his wealth of experience and knowledge to focus on innovation of the product.

David Bontoft, Managing Director, comments : "Our Company Vision Statement clearly indicates where the Company is going.

ACKNOWLEDGMENTS

The publisher would like to sincerely thank the following individuals and organisations for their help and contribution to this publication:

Andrew Fenton – Intertech

Mirropix

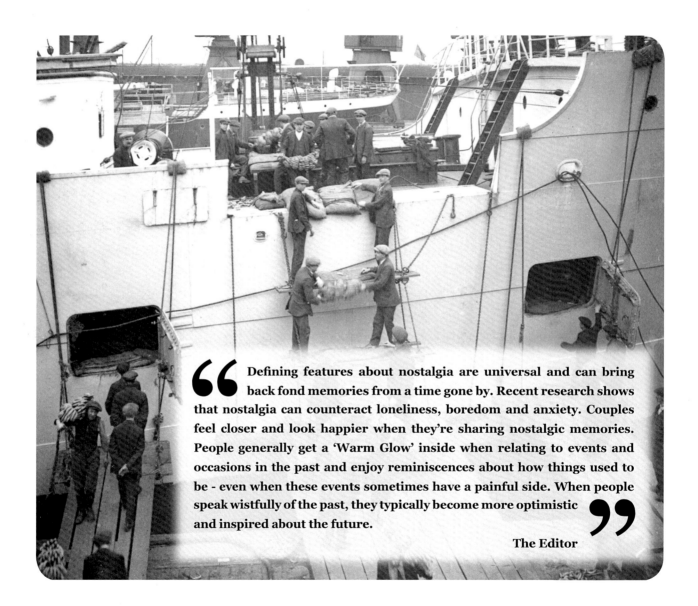

> Defining features about nostalgia are universal and can bring back fond memories from a time gone by. Recent research shows that nostalgia can counteract loneliness, boredom and anxiety. Couples feel closer and look happier when they're sharing nostalgic memories. People generally get a 'Warm Glow' inside when relating to events and occasions in the past and enjoy reminiscences about how things used to be - even when these events sometimes have a painful side. When people speak wistfully of the past, they typically become more optimistic and inspired about the future.
>
> **The Editor**